The Essential Buyer's Guide

JAGUAR

E-TYPE

Covers all models 1961 to 1971: 3.8 & 4.2-litre

T0169053

Your marque expert:
Peter Crespin

VELOCE PUBLISHING

THE PUBLISHER OF FINE AUTOMOTIVE BOOKS

Alfa Romeo Alfasud (Metcalfe)
Alfa Romeo Alfetta: all saloon/sedan models 1972 to 1984 & coupé models 1974 to 1987 (Metcalfe)
Alfa Romeo Giulia GT Coupé (Booker)
Alfa Romeo Giulia Spider (Booker)
Audi TT (Davies)
Audi TT Mk2 2006 to 2014 (Durnan)
Austin-Healey Big Healeys (Trummel)
BMW Boxer Twins (Henshaw)
BMW E30 3 Series 1981 to 1994 (Hosier)
BMW GS (Henshaw)
BMW X5 (Saunders)
BMW Z3 Roadster (Fishwick)
BMW Z4: E85 Roadster and E86 Coupé including M and Alpina 2003 to 2009 (Smitheram)
BSA 350, 441 & 500 Singles (Henshaw)
BSA 500 & 650 Twins (Henshaw)
BSA Bantam (Henshaw)
Choosing, Using & Maintaining Your Electric Bicycle (Henshaw)
Citroën 2CV (Paxton)
Citroën DS & ID (Heilig)
Cobra Replicas (Ayre)
Corvette C2 Sting Ray 1963-1967 (Falconer)
Datsun 240Z 1969 to 1973 (Newlyn)
DeLorean DMC-12 1981 to 1983 (Williams)
Ducati Bevel Twins (Falloon)
Ducati Desmodue Twins (Falloon)
Ducati Desmoquattro Twins – 851, 888, 916, 996, 998, ST4 1988 to 2004 (Falloon)
Fiat 500 & 600 (Bobbitt)
Ford Capri (Paxton)
Ford Escort Mk1 & Mk2 (Williamson)
Ford Focus RS/ST 1st Generation (Williamson)
Ford Model A – All Models 1927 to 1931 (Buckley)
Ford Model T – All models 1909 to 1927 (Barker)
Ford Mustang – First Generation 1964 to 1973 (Cook)
Ford Mustang – Fifth Generation (2005-2014) (Cook)
Ford RS Cosworth Sierra & Escort (Williamson)
Harley-Davidson Big Twins (Henshaw)
Hillman Imp (Morgan)
Hinckley Triumph triples & fours 750, 900, 955, 1000, 1050, 1200 – 1991-2009 (Henshaw)
Honda CBR FireBlade (Henshaw)
Honda CBR600 Hurricane (Henshaw)
Honda SOHC Fours 1969-1984 (Henshaw)
Jaguar E-Type 3.8 & 4.2 litre (Crespin)
Jaguar E-type V12 5.3 litre (Crespin)
Jaguar Mark 1 & 2 (All models including Daimler 2.5-litre V8) 1955 to 1969 (Thorley)
Jaguar New XK 2005-2014 (Thorley)
Jaguar S-Type – 1999 to 2007 (Thorley)
Jaguar X-Type – 2001 to 2009 (Thorley)
Jaguar XJ-S (Crespin)
Jaguar XJ6, XJ8 & XJR (Thorley)
Jaguar XK 120, 140 & 150 (Thorley)
Jaguar XK8 & XKR (1996-2005) (Thorley)
Jaguar/Daimler XJ 1994-2003 (Crespin)
Jaguar/Daimler XJ40 (Crespin)
Jaguar/Daimler XJ6, XJ12 & Sovereign (Crespin)
Kawasaki Z1 & Z900 (Orritt)
Land Rover Discovery Series 1 (1989-1998) (Taylor)
Land Rover Discovery Series 2 (1998-2004) (Taylor)
Land Rover Series I, II & IIA (Thurman)
Land Rover Series III (Thurman)
Lotus Elan, S1 to Sprint and Plus 2 to Plus 2S 130/5 1962 to 1974 (Vale)
Lotus Europa, S1, S2, Twin-cam & Special 1966 to 1975 (Vale)
Lotus Seven replicas & Caterham 7: 1973-2013 (Hawkins)
Mazda MX-5 Miata (Mk1 1989-97 & Mk2 98-2001) (Crook)
Mazda RX-8 (Parish)
Mercedes-Benz 190: all 190 models (W201 series) 1982 to 1993 (Parish)
Mercedes-Benz 280-560SL & SLC (Bass)

Mercedes-Benz G-Wagen (Greene)
Mercedes-Benz Pagoda 230SL, 250SL & 280SL roadsters & coupés (Bass)
Mercedes-Benz S-Class W126 Series (Zoporowski)
Mercedes-Benz S-Class Second Generation W116 Series (Parish)
Mercedes-Benz SL R129-series 1989 to 2001 (Parish)
Mercedes-Benz SLK (Bass)
Mercedes-Benz W123 (Parish)
Mercedes-Benz W124 – All models 1984-1997 (Zoporowski)
MG Midget & A-H Sprite (Horler)
MG TD, TF & TF1500 (Jones)
MGA 1955-1962 (Crosier)
MGB & MGB GT (Williams)
MGF & MG TF (Hawkins)
Mini (Paxton)
Morgan Plus 4 (Benfield)
Morris Minor & 1000 (Newell)
Moto Guzzi 2-valve big twins (Falloon)
New Mini (Collins)
Norton Commando (Henshaw)
Peugeot 205 GTI (Blackburn)
Piaggio Scooters – all modern two-stroke & four-stroke automatic models 1991 to 2016 (Willis)
Porsche 356 (Johnson)
Porsche 911 (964) (Streather)
Porsche 911 (991) (Streather)
Porsche 911 (993) (Streather)
Porsche 911 (996) (Streather)
Porsche 911 (997) – Model years 2004 to 2009 (Streather)
Porsche 911 (997) – Second generation models 2009 to 2012 (Streather)
Porsche 911 Carrera 3.2 (Streather)
Porsche 911SC (Streather)
Porsche 924 – All models 1976 to 1988 (Hodgkins)
Porsche 928 (Hemmings)
Porsche 930 Turbo & 911 (930) Turbo (Streather)
Porsche 944 (Higgins)
Porsche 981 Boxster & Cayman (Streather)
Porsche 986 Boxster (Streather)
Porsche 987 Boxster and Cayman 1st generation (2005-2009) (Streather)
Porsche 987 Boxster and Cayman 2nd generation (2009-2012) (Streather)
Range Rover – First Generation models 1970 to 1996 (Taylor)
Range Rover – Second Generation 1994-2001 (Taylor)
Range Rover – Third Generation L322 (2002-2012) (Taylor)
Reliant Scimitar GTE (Payne)
Rolls-Royce Silver Shadow & Bentley T-Series (Bobbitt)
Rover 2000, 2200 & 3500 (Marrocco)
Royal Enfield Bullet (Henshaw)
Subaru Impreza (Hobbs)
Sunbeam Alpine (Barker)
Triumph 350 & 500 Twins (Henshaw)
Triumph Bonneville (Henshaw)
Triumph Herald & Vitesse (Ayre)
Triumph Spitfire and GT6 (Ayre)
Triumph Stag (Mort)
Triumph Thunderbird, Trophy & Tiger (Henshaw)
Triumph TR2 & TR3 - All models (including 3A & 3B) 1953 to 1962 (Conners)
Triumph TR4/4A & TR5/250 - All models 1961 to 1968 (Child & Battyll)
Triumph TR6 (Williams)
Triumph TR7 & TR8 (Williams)
Triumph Trident & BSA Rocket III (Rooke)
TVR Chimaera and Griffith (Kitchen)
TVR S-series (Kitchen)
Velocette 350 & 500 Singles 1946 to 1970 (Henshaw)
Vespa Scooters – Classic 2-stroke models 1960-2008 (Paxton)
Volkswagen Bus (Copping)
Volkswagen Transporter T4 (1990-2003) (Copping/Cservenka)
VW Golf GTI (Copping)
VW Beetle (Copping)
Volvo 700/900 Series (Beavis)
Volvo P1800/1800S, E & ES 1961 to 1973 (Murray)

www.veloce.co.uk

First published in April 2006 by Veloce Publishing Limited, Veloce House, Parkway Farm Business Park, Middle Farm Way, Poundbury, Dorchester, Dorset, DT1 3AR, England. Reprinted September 2010, November 2014, February 2017 & November 2019. Tel: 01305 260068. Fax 01305 250479/ e-mail info@veloce.co.uk/web www.veloce.co.uk or www.velocebooks.com
ISBN: 978-1-787116-59-7 UPC: 6-36847-01659-3

Introduction & thanks
– the purpose of this book

Since the day it was first unveiled to an astonished Geneva audience in 1961, the E-type Jaguar has captivated not just car enthusiasts but also the public, with its incredibly graceful lines and stories of its 150mph performance. The E-type was truly ahead of its time and almost immediately became a byword for glamour, speed, and style. From the very outset, advertisers used the E-type in promoting their brands and the makers of model cars rapidly included it in their range, knowing it would appeal to daydreaming boys and probably their fathers too!

It would be almost forty years before I got my hands on a real E-type, but the dream never died. If you, like countless others, have always dreamt of owning an example of this true motoring icon, this book is for you. There are plenty of E-type histories, plenty of restoration books and lots of product catalogues. What has been lacking, until now, is a practical guide for people thinking of buying an E-type but wary of spending a large sum on an old car which could, quite literally, become more trouble than it is worth. Armed with this book's guidance you should be able to sort out the pretenders from the true concours-quality cars, the solid drivers from the lashed-together makeovers, and the realistic restoration projects from the hopeless basket cases. One thing is for sure, the E-type ownership experience is likely to be an emotional roller coaster unlike any other. Have fun!

Thanks
My sincere thanks go to all the E-type people I've met around the UK, USA and Europe since becoming an owner. I've enjoyed meeting all of them, staying with some and having others stay with me. Thanks, in particular, to the UK 'E-type Boys' and especially Angus Moss for his valuable help in checking and supplementing my work, Joe Hardy for help with 'community' information, and Dave Kerr for his unfailing support, all of whom also supplied photos for this book.

I also thank Marcus Arendt, Dave Ahlers, Jerry Mouton, Garth Nicholson, Graham and Fiona Heritage and Chuck Goolsbee for help with pictures. Last but by no means least, my dear wife, Dorothy, for her encouragement throughout.

Publisher's acknowledgement
We are indebted to Justin Banks who kindly supplied many of the images used in this book. Justin often has E-types for sale at www.justinbanks.com.

Contents

1 Is it the right car for you?
– marriage guidance

Tall and short drivers
The earliest E-types had flat floors, which make foot and leg room tight. Later cars had footwells, and a scalloped rear crossmember to permit more rearward seat movement. All bar the 2+2 from 1966 are short on headroom. Those with back problems/lack of mobility will find it hard to get in and out of an E-type as the doors are short and the seats very low: the 2+2 is better in this respect.

Weight of controls
The large steering wheel makes steering manageable, but wide tyres and/or a small steering wheel will increase effort. Some Series 2 cars have power steering. The clutch and throttle pedals are reasonable, but brake effort can be high – especially on 3.8 cars, or any E-type where the servo action or brake system is out of adjustment. Gear change is fine, although 3.8s need practice to achieve silent changes into first. Handbrake effort should be modest, but if the self-adjusting mechanism seizes or the pads glaze or get oily, then even a heavy pull won't hold the car.

Though under 6ft 1in (1.85m), the author would clearly have to squeeze below the soft top – if Dave Ahler's fine unfinished S2 had one, that is ...

Will it fit in the garage?
Series 1 & 2 Fixed Head Coupé (FHC) and Open Top Sports (OTS):

Length	4453mm/175.38in
Width	1656mm/65.25in (plus door opening room)

Series 1 & 2 2+2:

Length	4680mm/184.25in
Width	1656mm/65.25in

Interior space

The large steering wheel reduces thigh room, although some rake adjustment is possible.

There is room for two adults, although the tallest drivers will need to adapt and/or drive convertibles looking over the windscreen with the top down. All Series 1 E-types have steering reach and rake adjustment, the latter often forgotten. The 16in steering wheel makes thigh space tight for large drivers, and some very tall drivers bolt seats directly to the floor. The 2+2 cars have 9in longer doors, more head and leg room, and are much easier to get in and out of. Try before you buy. The 2+2 has extra space for two small people in the back or, more realistically, one person sitting sideways for short trips ...

Front seating is more roomy in the 2+2, and these rear seats will also hold one adult sideways for modest distances.

Luggage capacity

Convertibles can hold a few soft bags, but not much more, unless you fit a boot-top luggage rack. The FHC is much better, with a usable hatch and fold-down luggage restraint panel behind the seats, allowing space for a big suitcase and some soft bags. The 2+2 trumps them both with serious cargo space, if you choose to travel with a single passenger, as well as under-dash oddment trays. Rearward vision suffers on all models if heavily loaded.

The FHC offers good luggage room for a sporting car. The convertible's luggage space is less generous.

Running costs

These are classic cars and don't obey the normal rules of mass-produced motoring. Servicing follows usage and need, not a predetermined schedule. Expect oil changes around every 3-5000 miles, or yearly, whichever comes soonest, and budget for a refill of 6.25L or 11 pints (more than modern cars). Fuel consumption depends on driving style and gearing, but around 19-22mpg is average and covers most kinds of mixed motoring. Brake pads are not expensive but are fiddly to fit at the back, so either learn to do it or pay significant money for an expert.

Usability

A good standard E-type is very usable and should cope comfortably with city and open roads in all climates, although heating and ventilation are marginal in extremes of climate. An air conditioned car is useful in hot weather, but may increase load on the cooling system.

Parts availability

Most parts are available, many new. Excellent aftermarket and secondhand parts are a backup, but beware of shoddy quality and stick to sellers with a reputation to preserve, and a professional customer relations ethos. Many eBay items or other used spares are scrap, so buyers beware.

Parts cost

E-types are amongst the dearest mass-produced classics to restore, but much of that is labour-related. SU carburettors and triple manifolds are expensive, as are top-quality trim kits, many body and frame parts, and specialized items such as heated rear windows, hood frames and steering wheels. Much of the rest compares with other classic cars and may still be far cheaper than modern vehicles.

Insurance

More than some classics, but usually affordable for good risk drivers and sensible agreed values in reasonably insurable locations. Shop around and consider limited mileage and combined policies to keep costs down. Clubs often offer a discount. Consider insurance for the restoration phase, which can be risky and prolonged.

Investment potential
Good in terms of depreciation, poor in terms of making money from restoration. This is due to the high labour costs; a restored car is normally worth much less than the cost of repair. Do it for love and a hobby, not as a path to riches. Most of the barn finds have been found, and many of those have ruined their finders!

Failings
Precious few. The cars were outstanding in almost every respect in their day, so compared to every other classic (including Astons and Ferraris) an E-type is about as good as it gets, if you can get in and out and make yourself comfortable.

Plus points
Looks, power, refinement and handling, plus practicality in the case of the 2+2.

Minus points
Cost of restoration/repair, seats and gearbox in 3.8s, heating/ventilation in all models, lights in S1, and the brakes can be a little heavy. Rear brake access and cabin ergonomics are not great.

Alternatives (excluding expensive exotica)
Cobra replica, Alfa Romeo Giulia Spider/GT, Aston Martin DB4-6, Austin Healey 3000, Corvette, Daimler Dart, Jensen Interceptor, early Porsche 911, Sunbeam Tiger, Triumph TR4 and TR6, Datsun Z.

The author's E-type at rest and almost finished.

2 Cost considerations
– affordable, or a money pit?

Purchase

The cheapest E-type is rarely the best value, but many people cannot justify a high
price for a 'hobby' purchase. If you
want the very best car to enter shows
and perhaps win awards, you will need
to spend above £45,000. With little
more than regular servicing, a good
driver will cost around £18,000-30,000,
depending on the model. Both choices
mean you will spend significant money
initially, but comparatively little thereafter
on servicing and repairs. This way, the
cost of your E-type will consist of regular
loan repayments (for most people) for
an expensive car, but you will be using it
from day one.

An example of a good driver. Left hand
drive, this Series 1.5 should give many
years of enjoyment.

The alternative involves paying much less initially for a poor or incomplete car.
Then instead of making regular loan payments, you buy a steady stream of parts as
you build the vehicle yourself or pay a professional to do so. The ultimate cost will
be higher (unless you do most of the work yourself) but the advantage is that you
can slow down or stop, depending on finances, and you will have a hobby in the
meantime. However, be prepared to wait many years before your first drive ...

Beware of the third common route, which can be risky with E-types – that of
buying a car to drive after some light re-commissioning as a 'rolling restoration.'
The problem with E-types is that the most time and money are needed for the
body, which is rarely practical to repair
correctly while running the car. This
option can quickly turn into an expensive
way of buying a car which takes years to
be put properly back into commission.
The expression 'money pit' could have
been coined for E-types, since each
small problem uncovered rapidly leads to
more serious repair work, and so on ...

Servicing

Depends on time, rather than mileage
for little-used cars. Mostly DIY but
Jaguar or classic car specialists are
available for the more specialist tasks, if
needed.

A cheaper route is to buy a sound but
incomplete car. Joe Hardy's 'naked'
roadster has actually been completely
rebuilt and mostly lacks just interior trim,
hood and paint.

Job	Interval
Basic oil change	3000 miles/1 year
Annual service	6000 miles/1 year
Major service	18,000 miles/ 3 years
Adjust valve clearances	24,000 miles/ 5 yearly
Other	As needed

Much servicing can be done by the owner, and accessibility is excellent, apart from the rear brakes. Note the exquisite headers on Dave Kerr's car, courtesy of E-type Fabs.

Mechanical parts
Brake pads (S1) x15 axle set
Brake discs x25 each
Brake master cylinder:
x200 (4.2)/ x120 x 2 (3.8)
Brake servo x260 exchange (4.2)
Head gasket set x60
Gearbox rebuild x1500
Differential rebuild x1000
Fuel pump x40 (4.2)
Wheel set x1000
Exhaust system (stainless) x450-500
Tyres x80
Radiator x300
Clutch kit (plate, housing and release bearing) x170
Alternator x120
Water pump x100
Shock absorbers: rear (4 off) x25 each
Front (2 off) x60 each
Wiper motor x150 exchange
Fan motor x150 exchange
Thermostatic switch x15
SU carburettor rebuild kit x17 (3 off)
Starter motor x150

Bodywork
Bonnet complete new x4000-5000
Door skin x65
Windscreen x250
Convertible top x300
Convertible top frame, bare x1000
Rear wing x300
Bumper blade: front x125/rear x170
Over-riders: front x40/rear x45

Headlamp glass x75 x 2
Rear light cluster (S1) x120
Rear light (S2) x122
Bare-metal respray, average x3000
Fuel tank x250

Trim
Complete trim kit x1200 (excludes hood)
Refurbish steering wheel x50 (kit)
Dashboard top cover x60
Door cards x95 pair
Carpet set x160
New seat covers x480
Console trim kit (3.8) x110
Headlining x180 plus fitting

Used parts
Check magazines for dealers. Caution with eBay, as much E-type stuff is junk. Owner's club classifieds. Autojumbles/ swapmeets.

Occasionally an unfinished project comes onto the market. These can be a bargain if they are good. Angus Moss is not selling his, though.

3 Living with an E-type
– will you get along together?

Summary

E-types thrive on regular and energetic use. They're fast enough to beat almost every other classic car and many modern cars, yet give relaxed driving in difficult conditions. Provided you physically fit the car, the ergonomics are bearable and they are comfortable enough for long trips, with the possible exception of 3.8 seats. The cost of fuel will be significant, but not terrible. You'll find the car delivers everything you might want of it, save large amounts of luggage room in convertibles. Try before you buy, but once hooked you may find you can't live without an E-type.

Long journeys are perfectly feasible in an E-type, although ear plugs are advisable with the top down. Chuck Goolsbee's car in typically moody pose.

Good points
• Every trip is a special occasion!
• One of the most beautiful and respected cars in the world.
• The view over the bonnet.
• Incredible torque, overall performance and good handling.
• Acceleration at speed.
• Long distances are not a problem.
• Excellent ride quality for a fast car.
• Excellent forward visibility due to narrow screen pillars.
• Excellent front and rear crumple zones.
• Most servicing can be DIY.
• The 2+2 is superbly practical.
• Power steering, air conditioning and automatic all available.
• Excellent spares availability.
• Lots of performance options and scope for personalisation.

Bad points
• Cost of purchase/rebuilding.
• Fuel consumption.
• Seat adjustment in early cars.
• Seat comfort of 3.8s on long journeys.
• Headroom for tall drivers (except 2+2).
• Braking effort.
• Tricky first gear change (3.8).
• Heating and ventilation in extremes of weather.
• Cost of some specialist parts.
• Cost or hassle of some basic jobs such as rear brake work.
• Lights on Series 1 cars and poor wipers at very high speed.
• Security, for such a valuable car.
• Susceptibility to structural corrosion.
• Reliability of original electrical parts.
• Overheating in traffic for questionable cars in hot climates.
• Low ground clearance.
• Modest luggage space.
• Many poor or over-priced cars.

If this view moves you, let alone the 200-plus horsepower from the lusty XK, you will surely get along with an E-type.

4 Relative values
– which model for you?

E-types vary greatly in basic character, so normally people go for the model type they want and cost considerations are secondary. If, on the other hand, cost itself is the major determinant, below are some approximate relative values, with the dearest as 100% and others shown as a percentage of that value. Note, however, that outside latch and even flat floor models are scarce, so 'real world' comparisons should exclude those. Also, in some markets, the most sought after cars can be 4.2 models because they are easier to live with than 'purer' 3.8s. The lightweight models or bona fide historic competition cars are excluded from this list.

Series 1 3.8 'Outside latch' (rare first models) .. 100%
Series 1 3.8 'Flat floor' convertible 85%
Series 1 3.8 'Flat floor' FHC. 80%
Series 1 3.8 convertible 75%
Series 1 3.8 FHC 60%
Series 1 4.2 convertible 70%
Series 1 4.2 FHC 55%
Series 1 2+2* 40%
Series 1.5 convertible 65%
Series 1.5 FHC 50%
Series 1.5 2+2* 35%
Series 2 convertible 60%
Series 2 FHC 45%
Series 2 2+2* 30%

Automatics (always long-wheelbase cars), even clean S1 cars like this, are the lowest price E-types like-for-like, due to sluggish demand.

*Automatic models normally worth circa 5-10% less, depending on condition. All values will vary by condition and market.

In the UK, the 4.2 Series 1 cars are considered to have the best combination of desirability and practicality. The 3.8s appeal most to the purists and do command good prices. Series 2 cars are cheaper, although they are perfectly good (some would say the best) regular drivers. In all markets, cars with anything other than triple SU carbs are worth significantly less. Series 1.5 cars were never officially a separate series and there is dispute about what constitutes an S1.5. Basically, they were S1s with early-style open headlights, not protruding quite as far as on the later S2, and usually with the S2 cooling system and revised centre dash. They are hard to price, but from the back look like an S1 so they can fetch slightly better money than an S2.

Even in the wettest climates, convertible cars tend to command top price and 2+2 cars cost less than either the convertible or FHC versions. However, beware of a 2+2 described as an FHC, sometimes intentionally to justify a higher price.

5 Before you view
– be well informed

To avoid the frustration of a car not matching your expectations, be sure to ask specific questions when you call before viewing. Excitement about buying an E-type can make even obvious things slip your mind, and it's harder for sellers to answer very specific questions dishonestly. Try to assess the attitude and demeanour of the seller, and decide how comfortable you are buying a used car from him or her.

Where is the car?
Work out the cost of travelling to view a car. For a rare model, or the exact specification you want, it may be worth travelling but if your target is a common vehicle, decide first how far you're prepared to go. Locally advertised cars can add to your knowledge for very little effort, so pay them a visit if possible.

Dealer or private sale
Is the seller the owner or a trader? Private owners should have all the history and be happy to answer detailed questions. Dealers may know less about a car but should have some documentation and may offer finance. If a dealer offers no warranty or guarantee in writing, then consider if it's worth paying their higher price for no better guarantee than with a cheaper private sale.

Cost of collection and delivery
Dealers may deliver, but it probably won't be cheap. Private owners may meet you halfway, especially if the car is roadworthy, but be sure to view the car at the vendor's address beforehand to validate ownership and vehicle documentation.

Viewing – when and where?
It's always preferable to view at the vendor's home or business. A private seller's name and address should be on the title documents unless there's a good reason why not. Have at least one viewing in daylight and preferably dry weather. Most cars look better in poor light or when wet.

Reason for sale
Genuine sellers will explain why they are selling and their length of ownership. They may also know something about previous owners.

Conversions and specials
Many E-types have returned to Europe from the USA. Conversion to RHD normally reduces their absolute value but makes them more saleable in the UK. Conversion can be easily verified as ID number sequences differed between RHD and LHD.
   Check if headlamps, wiper pattern and sidelamp colour are correct for your market, as some safety inspections insist on this. Ask about the carburettors and

A pointer to a converted LHD car is wipers parking on the passenger side.

Ask if the interior is original. These boards look good but are not standard and hurt the car's value. The hatch seal is the wrong way round.

pistons, because US market Series 2 cars were given power-sapping twin Strombergs and anti-emissions equipment, often mated to low-compression engines. They also had extra side lights which spoil the clean lines. Switch and gauge orientation also differed on LHD cars, but is often left unchanged because conversion takes time and money.

Condition (body/chassis/interior/mechanics)

Query the car's condition in as specific terms as possible – preferably citing the checklist items described in Chapter 9.

Ask if the car has 'matching numbers' which correspond with its data plate.

All original specification

An unmolested original car is invariably of higher value and easier to get spares for than a customised vehicle.

Matching data/legal ownership

E-types have a chassis number, body number, engine number and gearbox number. All the numbers on the major parts and data plate should match to justify a top price, although changed engines, etc, noted on registration documents are acceptable, especially if the originals come with the car.

Does the vendor own the car outright or is money owed to a finance company or bank? Might the car be stolen? Do any necessary finance checks before buying. Such companies can often also confirm if the car has ever been an insurance write-off.

In the UK, the following organisations can supply vehicle data:

DVSA	0300 123 9000
HPI	0845 300 8905
AA	0344 209 0754
DVLA	0844 306 9203
RAC	0800 015 6000

Other countries will have similar organisations.

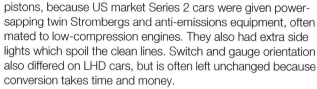

Many ex-US cars have only twin carbs, although these are not the normal 'Stranglebergs.'

Roadworthiness
Does the car have all necessary certificates and/or comply with emissions rules?

Test status for UK cars can be checked by phoning 0845 600 5977. Similar checks are available in some other markets.

If required, does the car carry a current road fund licence/license plate tag?

Unleaded fuel
All E-types have hardened valve seats suited to unleaded fuel. Treat as suspect any claims of so-called 'unleaded conversions.'

Insurance
If intending to drive the car home, check with your existing insurer in case your current policy does not cover you. It's wise to check insurance costs before purchase in any case, as E-types are valuable and fast cars.

How you can pay
A cheque/check will take several days to clear and the seller may prefer to sell to a cash buyer. Cash can also be a valuable bargaining tool. However, a banker's draft or money order may be as good as cash, so ask beforehand.

Buying at auction?
See Chapter 10.

Professional vehicle check
E-types are complex fast cars and some important checks need to be made. There are often marque/model specialists who will undertake professional examination of a vehicle on your behalf. Owner's clubs will be able to put you in touch with such specialists.

Other organisations that will carry out a general professional check in the UK are:

AA   0800 056 8040 (motoring organisation with vehicle inspectors)
RAC   0330 159 0720 (motoring organisation with vehicle inspectors)
Other countries will have similar organisations.

6 Inspection equipment
– these items will really help

This book
Glasses (if needed)
Magnet (not powerful, a fridge magnet is ideal)
Torch
Probe (a small screwdriver works very well)
Overalls
Mirror on a stick
Digital camera
A friend, preferably a knowledgeable enthusiast

Don't leave home without them. Magnet, mirror, torch and probe.

This book is designed to be your guide at every step, so take it along and use the check boxes in Chapter 9 to help assess each area. Don't be afraid to let the seller see you using it.

Take your reading glasses if you need them to read documents and make close-up inspections. Seems obvious, but it's too late to remember your close-up eyewear when you drive up to the vendor's premises.

A magnet will help you check if the car is full of filler, or has fibreglass panels, but be careful not to damage the paintwork. It is a rule of E-types that the rust you see is always far less than the hidden rust you cannot see. There's nothing wrong with a fibreglass bonnet or boot lid apart from the lowered value and sometimes paint finish, but the rest of the body on an E-type is structural and must be sound metal. Very occasionally an E-type, especially one with some track history, may have alloy panels such as doors, bonnet or boot lid, and these will not be magnetic. However, in such cases, the owner will probably boast about these expensive parts.

A small screwdriver can be used – with care – as a probe, particularly on the inner and outer sills, rear lower quarters, boot floor, and anywhere around the bulkhead and battery tray to check any areas of corrosion.

Be prepared to get dirty and preferably take some overalls for getting under these low cars. Fixing a mirror at an angle on the end of a stick can help check the condition of the underside of the car and some of the important areas around the front frames and their attachment points. You can also use it, together with the torch, along the underside of the sills and deep inside the footwells to check the floor and inner sills. A full on-ramp inspection is ideal.

If possible, take a digital camera for reference or to study known trouble spots later. Take a picture of the data plate and use the information to search for the car or its near cousins on www.xkedata.com, which may reveal valuable history. Also, show pictures of any part of the car that causes you concern to an expert for comment. Ideally, have a friend or knowledgeable enthusiast accompany you: a second opinion is always valuable, especially from somebody not spending their own money.

E-types have sold on looks since launch in 1961, so falling in love at first sight is all too likely, especially if this is your first viewing. E-types in the flesh look even lower and sleeker than in photos, and are so seductive it's hard not to overlook flaws in your urge to own such a beautiful piece of automobile art. Even a rough one can captivate you and seem to whisper, 'Buy me and clean me and I'll make you so proud.'

Faced with emotional and logical reasons why you simply have to buy one of these rolling sculptures, you need a tough carapace of equal parts scepticism and factual knowledge about what to look for, to judge the car's true condition. This chapter will help decide whether a car should make it onto your shortlist and justify taking your inspection further. There is only one serious alternative to learning all about E-types before looking at one: beg, borrow or pay for the time of somebody who already knows how to judge these unique cars.

Your initial check should cover the basics such as the paperwork. The rest will vary depending on what type of car you are looking for.

Concours contender
If you are paying top money for a supposed concours car, you ought to be able to take many aspects for granted, pending more detailed checks later, and spend your fifteen minutes seeing if the car really has those special features that justify the price.

Clean but no prize-winner. Modern cable ties, no mudshield rubber and no black battery.

To be certain how 'correct' a car is, you would need an experienced concours judge and/or detailed reference to concours guidelines, such as those published by the Jaguar Clubs of North America. Buying a car with a history of winning top awards (not just local car shows) is another method. Although the checks needed to verify condition are legion, and some judging schemas ignore entire aspects of the car, such as suspension components, the following guide points should establish if the car is a serious contender or not. There is no space to publish exhaustive judging criteria and you may have to do a little research to establish what is correct for 'your' car.

Perfect bonnet seams but variable bonding quality for glued panels.

Under the bonnet
Assuming the major components such as the engine, radiator, and frame rails, etc, are standard,

the devil is in the detail. For example, are all the vacuum hoses correct cloth braided type? Are the brake reservoir hoses correct with a yellow stripe? Do the reservoirs have filters inside? Are the water and other hose clamps the correct Cheney or Jubilee brand, not modern stainless? Are the throttle linkages and brackets correct cadmium plate? Do the hydraulic cylinders have the original date tags?

A 3.8 coverted to negative earth. Wrong air cleaners are obvious, hex-head hose clamps less so.

Are all fasteners the right type – with the special 'long' Nylocs on the frame fixings? Is the harness correctly cloth covered, held by the correct plastic strapping (not cable ties) and with a period hard rubber battery fitted? Are the electrical items correctly date-stamped with correct decals? Is the original Lucas-type dynamo (3.8) or alternator (4.2) fitted, with correct shields over the latter and a 'Negative Earth' plate on the heater box on Series 1 cars?

Are the exhaust manifolds correctly enamelled and suspension joints fitted with grease nipples, not sealed for life? Are the suspension rubbers original matt black or incorrect modern shiny polymer material? Are discs and calipers the original type and the water shields present (4.2)? Is the data plate an original etched type or a screen-printed reproduction? Is the fuel filter correct and are all bulkhead grommets present and the correct type?

Garth Nicholson's super-clean 4.2 car with correct mudshields, frequently missing (although they should be black).

Is the wiper motor harness connector clamp present? Is the headlamp (and cabin) glass correctly Triplex marked? Is the felt seal present over the radiator stoneguard and the alloy shield present below? Are the torsion bars' shields present if required, with the correct fabric strip and factory aluminium strip clamps? Are the bonnet hinges body colour with black springs and the brass washers at the pivots (S1)? Are all three SU carb damper tops the same, and numbered AUC 8115? Do the carbs have their tags and are they in the right place? Is the fuel rail correct with a screwed union to the flex pipe, and are the coil, spark plug conduit and plug caps correct?

Body and interior

Are the wiper blades and steering wheel spokes polished (S1) or satin (S2)? Is the horn inset trim ring chrome (S1) or black (S2)? Does the soft top on a convertible have the lead shot bag sewn in and a duck green frame? Is the gear lever gaiter the correct leatherette material or rubber moulding for the model, with the correct ferrule on the former? Is the dash top the correct moulding or creased DIY vinyl? Are the under-dash panels and map light present and correct? Is the rev counter redlined at 5500rpm (3.8) or 5000rpm (4.2) with or without a working clock (S1)?

Is the radio a period item, with speaker(s) invisible behind the console sides? Is the interior trim held with invisible clips or incorrect visible screws? Are the headlight trim screws slotted head (3.8) or Pozidriv (4.2) and the correct PL type headlamps used for the 3.8? Is the bumper rubber trim mounted with the beaded edge invisible? Are the wheels curly hub (S1) or smooth (S2)? Are the exhaust resonators the short type (3.8), longer type (4.2) or curved (S2)?

This '65 car should have a rubber bulb gearshift gaiter, not this mess!

Is the boot or tailgate seal correctly fitted, allowing the panel to sit flush? Are the boot boards (4.2) or foldable cover (3.8) correctly fitted? Is the toolkit present and correct, with Thor knock-off hammer if appropriate? Is the jack present and of the right type? Is the original in-tank fuel pump present (3.8) or an SU type (4.2) with white nylon fuel lines?

Are the panel gaps good with flat and level bumpers and over-rider faces perpendicular to the ground? Are the rear lamp lenses and reflectors the correct colour for your market and Lucas brand rather than aftermarket? Are the shock absorbers original pattern and the halfshaft universal joint covers fitted (4.2)? If all these items check out and the provenance is good, the car is at least fair and worth checking thoroughly.

An early 3.8 but fitted with some 4.2-type console parts and trim, and missing a pedal rubber.

Daily driver

The fifteen minute check for a moderately priced car should concentrate on the fundamentals. These should be checked for the concours car too of course, but are less likely to be in dispute for a top car and reputable seller. You need to be more cautious if buying a mid-price car privately or from a general classic trader.

Clear indicator lenses are correct for the USA but not other markets.

Do the numbers on the data plate even match the car's components? The engine number is stamped on the block either above the oil filter or, on late engines, at the back on the left bell flange. Early engines also had the number stamped on the head behind the timing chain in the cam box valley. The chassis number is on the right side of the front transverse engine frame ('picture frame'), above the shock absorber mount. The gearbox and body numbers are harder to check quickly, but if a manual 2+2 has a chassis number ending in BW, then it was originally an automatic, so that at least shows a non-original transmission. Be aware of ground-off numbers and fake re-stamps. All of the checks under the next heading apply too.

Rough but complete

With E-types, more than perhaps any mass-produced classic, you simply must take extreme care to inspect the bodywork as closely as possible. This is the most expensive, time consuming and skill-dependent aspect of the car to rectify if it is in poor condition. It is far better to purchase a car with suspect mechanicals in a confirmed good body, than take on a structurally questionable E-type with good running gear.

Poor detailing on a sound car. Door seals protruding, bumper seal loose, and crumpled radiator intake.

When examining a good daily driver or a rough but running car, the key is to assume nothing and to check everything. Two cars in apparently similar condition can vary hugely, and one which appears in fair condition can actually be in far worse repair than another which looks much scruffier. Being methodical and working through the following check list will give you a quick overall snapshot of the car's condition.

Under the bonnet, does all look tidy and corrosion free? Does the bonnet hold itself open and look dent free from inside as well as outside, showing no filler has been used?

Does the car have the correct E-type engine or at least one from another Jaguar? Walk away from any car with a non-Jaguar engine, especially if the frames have been cut or the transmission tunnel savaged. Assuming a Jaguar XK engine is fitted, does it sport the correct carburettors for its age and market? Triple SUs were used for all UK and most export cars except almost all North American spec Series 1.5 and certainly S2 cars, which used twin Strombergs with cast alloy or pressed steel crossover ducts to special exhaust manifolds. Are the correct fibreglass air plenum and filter canister still present? Some late S2 cars with Strombergs used slim steel filter cases similar to the

This bulkhead rusted through due to a dripping heater pipe inside.

XJ6 type, with a flexible crossover hot air intake pipe connected to a pressed steel exhaust heat shield.

On the inside, is the trim more or less to spec and in good condition? Does it smell of leather or mould, indicating a water leak? Does it look neglected or cared for (as opposed to polished merely for sale)? Do the windows work and is the glass clear or scratched? Do all the electrics work, especially the wipers, and does the fan come on when the engine warms up?

Try to see as much of the underside as possible – the floor and chassis rails should be body colour over stonechip paint, although good underseal is acceptable. Use your fridge magnet to check the outside of the sills for filler – especially in front of and behind the doors, where the body panels meet the bulkheads. Also use your fridge magnet to check around the wheel arches, and the vulnerable front and rear corners where the lights are attached.

A scruffy but basically sound boot floor. Note the front tank mount holes which must have the reinforcing plate mounted behind them.

If buying a project car, try for one where the worst corrosion has been repaired, such as this battery area.

The boot floor at the back and bonnet undertray at the front are both prone to scraping, subsequent rusting and perforation from both inside and outside. Inspect them closely and be sceptical of underseal here as elsewhere.

Look at the tyres for unusual wear patterns indicating suspension problems. Look for leaks from the differential output and input seals, and the back of the engine at the cam feed or the bell housing below.

If the car starts, first press the brakes and see if the pedal moves further as soon as the engine runs. This will indicate if the servo is working. On test, the car should run straight and true with no strange noises and not pull to one side under braking or acceleration. The normal road test tips apply about checking for smoke on acceleration or the overrun, clunks, rattles, wheel bearing noises, etc.

Many E-types are sold as recent imports or 'barn finds' awaiting restoration. Their pricing varies from the realistic to the ridiculously optimistic, but in all cases it is almost certain that the cost of the car, plus a reasonable restoration, will be far more than the price of a car in good condition to begin with. If, however, your funds simply do not stretch to a good car, or you are looking specifically for a long-term restoration project, then they may be worthy of consideration, provided you have no illusions about the time and resources you will need to finish the job.

At least with obvious restoration candidates, the faults are usually on display. Even so, beware of the over-optimistic assumption that the damage you see is the damage you will need to fix. By the time an E-type looks visibly poor, much of the body shell may be scrap, and restoration will be a far more complex and costly task than you envisage. This has to be reflected in a rock-bottom price, unless the car is anything other than an ultra rare flat-floor or outside bonnet latch vehicle, or one with proven exceptional competition or historical significance. Keep any original components you replace.

Peeling back carpets and scraping can reveal true horror stories like this. A 2+2 rear inner sill.

This is the bottom of a 2+2 screen pillar, of all places. Not somewhere you might think to check. Even the roof on this car needed new metal!

As mentioned elsewhere, the single biggest aspect to check when buying an E-type is bodywork condition. Jaguar didn't expect the E-type to be a particularly big seller, let alone last fifty-plus years, so longevity did not figure in design considerations. In any case, body rust proofing was in its infancy.

The key points to consider when buying an E-type are:

Avoid repaired frames. This one is not even brazed but welded.

Beware frame rust. The high tensile tubing was never expected to last so many years. This frame is scrap. Most original ones are by now.

- Structural bodywork
- Cosmetic bodywork
- Interior trim
- Engine and gearbox
- Suspension and brakes
- Instruments and electrics

Paradoxically, the biggest problems with E-types – structural and cosmetic rust – are exacerbated by what is literally their biggest strength, ie the large monocoque box sections. These massively stiff fabricated sill channels and the front and rear bulkheads, are complemented by an enclosed transmission tunnel and cross stiffeners, calculated to give race car handling in the convertible, with the fixed head coupé version benefiting in terms of weather protection but not significantly in terms of torsional rigidity. The handling objective was amply achieved, but left the design prone to internal condensation and therefore rust.

You therefore need to check the type and extent of corrosion and can take it for granted that there will be some, unless the car has very recently been fully restored and rust-proofed, with photographic evidence. Even restored cars rust and a few years is long enough for condensation to take hold once more, especially if storage conditions have been questionable. Concrete floors in particular sweat significant moisture and in a poorly ventilated garage – mistakenly regarded as weatherproof – this can play havoc with internal structures. The box sections and doors are provided with air gaps to act as drains but as well as letting water out, they can, of course, allow vapour in.

This perforated sill is typical of damage around the battery area.

Bubbling under paint is always a sign of expensive repairs on an E-type.

21

The complex stiffeners behind apparently simple panels show how important it is to buy an E-type with sound bodywork.

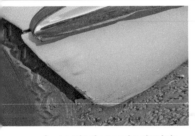

A seemingly good paint job can hide horrors such as this disintegrating front undertray.

This sort of surface rust is no serious threat, however.

A recent paint job is not a guarantee that the steel panels underneath are, or will remain, in good condition. The original bodies were lead-loaded, a labour-intensive skilled technique for smoothing seams and imperfections, which at least has the advantage of being totally watertight. Many old fillers are porous and consequently a source of slow corrosion under the paintwork.

Cosmetic as opposed to structural bodywork, comprises the chrome trim and closures – ie the rear hatch or boot lid, doors and bonnet, plus convertible hood or sunroof if present. All of it is easily examined for rust and fit. The bonnet comprises a large part of the bodywork and can be inspected from both sides.

The interior of an E-type was luxurious compared to its rivals, and Jaguar always referred to the car as a Grand Tourer rather than a sports car. The trim level and materials reflected this. Consequently, E-types are expensive cars to retrim to a high standard and previous owners often inflict poor DIY trim. Check the interior for musty smells and fluid leaks from the clutch and brake cylinders, which will ruin the carpet and paint in the driver's footwell.

The engine and gearbox, whilst large and heavy, are not unduly complex, although some expertise is required to work on the cylinder head in particular. Most parts are long-lasting and readily available, so unless you are looking at a total rebuild by a professional workshop, the engine is likely to be serviceable at modest cost for at least some time if it runs well.

The front and rear suspension, and in particular their pivots and mounting points, inevitably corrode and wear unless meticulously maintained. They also require some expertise and special tools to service or repair. The differential is hugely strong and unless it runs dry or is badly neglected, is normally good for further work, even if the limited slip clutch has worn somewhat. Brakes on the other hand – particularly the difficult to service rear discs – are often in poor shape, especially for such a potent car. The difficulty of working on them means that often it is easiest to repair or replace entire systems rather than

A worrying amount of filler around an apparently small blemish, but in an important place.

The paint job from hell. Not much being hidden here at least.

Even rebuilt cars have problems. This new anti-roll bar link fell apart on Willem Kemper's car.

do piecemeal repairs. This costs a lot, so pay special attention to condition and look for leaking differential oil on the discs, for example.

E-type electrics are another weak point so many years on, so check everything works and that the battery charges and oil pressure is good. The clocks set into Series 1 rev counters are normally broken by now, but can be repaired with modern electronics. Look under the bonnet and inside the car at the general condition and tidiness of the wiring.

Not perfect, but a very solid bonnet and good for many years to come with care, apart from the undertray.

9 Serious evaluation

– 60 minutes for years of enjoyment

This more searching examination will not only confirm if the car is worth buying, but will almost certainly show up a few areas of weakness to use as bargaining points. Circle the excellent, good, average or poor box for each check and add up the points at the end. Be realistic in your assessment and remember to be especially vigilant where body or frame checks are concerned. Use your magnet to check for filler and some kind of pointer probe to check for thin metal or perforation, but don't jack up the car on the sump or thin metal.

Exterior and running gear

Ex 4 Gd 3 Av 2 Po 1

This S2 has an excellent stance. Level, not sagging – it looks fresh and ready to go.

How does the car stand? Flat and even is correct, with a very slight nose-down stance acceptable, especially with low fuel level. Any sideways sag or down-at-heel stance means tired springs or badly adjusted torsion bars. Cars with fibreglass or alloy bonnets need to have the torsion bars reset to compensate for the reduction in sprung weight.

Body ripples

Ex 4 Gd 3 Av 2 Po 1

A good E-type should have flowing undistorted horizontal reflections in the bodywork, so try to park next to railings or fencing to give a reference line. Look especially for creases near the front of the doors or the rear of the bulkhead sides, and look for distortion along the bottom door edges or near the wheel arches. Car park dings will leave typical short vertical creases and are unsightly, but not indicative of serious damage. The sills should be straight and true for the whole length, with good body colour, sometimes over stone chip paint.

Underside and sills

Ex 4 Gd 3 Av 2 Po 1

This should be body colour over stone chip. The same finish applies to the boot floor, which should be solid, and the bonnet undertray which frequently shows signs of scraping and physical or rust perforation. The small hole at the front of the undertray is for the USA license plate swivel rod and is normal. The outer sills

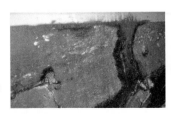

See how this front sill drain is almost totally invisible, covered in underseal over the new metalwork. Blocked drains mean rotted sills, new or old.

See the large dent in the footwell and damage around the central jacking point.

A jack and hood cover are always worth having – these items are for the later OTS models.

They don't come much better underneath than Garth Nicholson's 4.2.

should be a single continuous sheet, with several drain slots at the lower sill seam and no filler. Sometimes over-exuberant use of underseal blocks the drain holes, leading to rust which the owner was trying to avoid.

Bonnet/hood

Ex	Gd	Av	Po
4	3	2	1

This accounts for 35% of the bodywork and should be steel, not fibreglass or aluminium, on an original car. Check inside condition and beware of underseal, except in wheel arches. Are the air ducts, headlight and wheel arch diaphragm panels solidly bonded to the outer skin? Are the diaphragms rusted or the headlight buckets perforated or the bonnet seams rough? Does the bonnet close in line with the wheel arches? Is there rust around the hinge? Run your hand inside the front air intake opening and feel for filler or bent metal. E-type wheel arches are formed by the sheet metal being rolled over wire to give a characteristic rounded feel and stiff edge, so check for rust or poor repairs.

A typical S2 bonnet in good, not fantastic, shape. There's nothing wrong with a car used regularly and it is easy to check for damage.

Boot/trunk lid or hatch

Ex	Gd	Av	Po
4	3	2	1

This is a difficult item, being fettled to fit the individual car, so make sure the gaps are good and that it is dent free. Has it been fitted with a boot rack? Is there evidence of water leaking into the boot via the boot lid? The rear hatch is identical on fixed heads or 2+2 cars, and apart from checking for stripped hinge bolts and missing trim or rust in the seams, there is not much to go wrong.

Engine frames

Ex	Gd	Av	Po
4	3	2	1

The front frames should be body colour with no evidence of repair or damage. Knock the frames and listen for rust flakes falling down the diagonal tubes. Inspect closely around the front suspension and engine mounts for evidence of kinking, cracking or patching. Not even slight pinhole rusting is acceptable. At the front, the rectangular cross frame or picture frame is often damaged through careless jacking. Lightly twisted edges are not terminal, but any separating of the bottom inverted 'U' from the sides of the box section is serious. The bonnet support frame bends severely if used as a jacking point and can easily dent the underside of the bonnet as the radiator is forced upward.

Floors

Ex Gd Av Po
4 3 2 1

Lift the carpets to check the floors and inner sills for rust. There should be various plugs in place and no holes. Check where the floor meets the various stiffening crossmembers, transmission tunnel and the front/rear bulkheads. Check the transmission tunnel has not been cut to do bodged transmission work. Check footwell seams on all but the earliest flat-floor cars, and behind the seats check for rust or patching where the radius arms attach to the floor, as this is an important safety area, as are seat belt mounts.

Be sure to lift the carpets to check the floor. Many are paper-thin.

Front bulkhead

Ex Gd Av Po
4 3 2 1

This is critical for body shell integrity, so pay special attention from inside the car and under the bonnet, to the area around the battery where the left frame fastens to the vertical bulkhead as it often rusts or gets patched. The battery bracket should support a plastic tray under the battery, with a drain hose to below sill level. The right side bulkhead also suffers, but usually not as badly. Look for any rippling or other crash damage where the frames attach. Some bulkheads have been cut for non-standard transmissions or heaters, etc. Carefully prise any grommets free and shine a torch inside. The ID plate is held by four rivets on the right bulkhead (left on S2), and it is usually obvious if it has been tampered with.

Is it any wonder bulkheads corrode? Shine your torch into any open grommet holes to check for corrosion.

Doors

Ex Gd Av Po
4 3 2 1

Check the door gaps and hinge drop. Even reskinned doors may have bad frames as they are hard to repair/ replace. Doors should fit flush and snug with a thud, not a clang. Run your hand along the base and front underside where corrosion is worst, and check the three drain slots are open and the sill seal deflectors are present over each to let the water escape when the doors are shut. At the front of the doors there should be an uncorroded drip tray with a drain tube into the door cavity, and if the door cards are removed, check the sheet metal drip shields are present to protect the winder and door latch mechanisms.

This kind of underseal is obviously covering good metal. It is not always the case.

Rear quarters and spare wheel well

Ex Gd Av Po
4 3 2 1

The rear arches and chassis rails are prime corrosion sites and complex to repair. Feel for non-standard panel seams and overlaps inside the wheel arch and rear quarters and look for signs of welded patches, which probably hide serious further corrosion internally. The spare wheel well can fill with water and rot from inside. Be sceptical of thick underseal and probe well. The front boot floor section often lacks the four-bolt stiffener, which is fiddly to refit single-handed, but braces the central front fuel tank mount. Look under the car to see if it is missing or the panel distorted.

Convertible top

Ex [4] Gd [3] Av [2] Po [1]

Check the folding action, the condition of the material, and presence of full sealing components and hood catches. There is a one-side-first technique for closing the roof catches but no undue force should be needed. Rear window and chrome trim condition are important, and the presence of the anti-drum bag of lead shot is a good feature. Check the condition of the hood frame and fasteners, and also that the window cannot be wound up higher than the rubber seal on the hood frame. A separate hard top – preferably fully trimmed and with a clear unmisted or yellowed plastic rear window – is a definite plus, as these are rare and expensive.

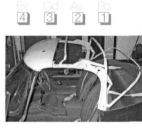

Most hood frames are nothing like as clean as this. Check carefully.

Paint

Ex [4] Gd [3] Av [2] Po [1]

E-types were amongst the first cars to use acrylic paint, but five-plus decades later, this means little. Due to their value, many E-types will have undergone a bare metal respray. If the paint is poor, prepare for a commensurate bill of your own. Look for signs of overspray on rubber seals, a poor finish inside the filler flap and recess, inside the spare wheel well and the door returns. See also Chapter 14.

Lights & body trim

Ex [4] Gd [3] Av [2] Po [1]

Three types of rear light exist for Series 1 or 1.5, being subtly different for OTS, FHC and 2+2 cars. Body filler is sometimes used to match them to the body contours, which is wrong. Check for pitting on expensive lamp bodies front and rear, and look for good rubber gasket fit and undamaged lenses with no moisture collection, especially on the low-slung S2 lights. Check for an undistorted stainless rear lamp panel and on all cars look for uncorroded and watertight reversing and number plate lamps. Bumpers should be solidly fixed and level, with the correct flush-fitting rubber bead, no droop, and vertical undamaged over-riders with no holes from AMCO bars. The long thin windscreen chromes, rear and side window and gutter chromes, are expensive and tricky to fit, so check all are present and not held on by bodged self-tapping screws. Modern replacements often do not fit well. Headlamp chrome trim should be smooth and undistorted, with no gasket bulging out or corrosion around screw holes. Check the multi-pin bonnet electrical plug and that the harness is not binding on the bonnet frame.

Absolutely perfect lamp fit to body. Bumper trim less good.

Typical seals for a daily driver. All present but starting to come slightly adrift in several places.

Body seals

The E-type's refinement at speed comes from effective sealing. FHC/2+2 window frames have a thin blade all along the top and front that seals against the screen pillar and gutter. They also have a channel felt seal to avoid wind whistle or window rattle. The body should have either a complex moulded seal running all the way from the bottom front of the door up the 'A' post and along the roof to the 'B' post (FHC), or a bulb-type seal on 2+2 models, held in a riveted channel. Boot seals for convertibles may hold the lid proud but rather than search for a better seal, the solution is normally to adjust the body flange it clips to.

In the case of rear hatches, the problem is likely to be an incorrectly fitted seal which can be mounted over the channel rather than in it. In all cases, the rear boot or hatch seal must not obscure the drain hole(s) for the channel. The bonnet is sealed by a bulb seal at the back in a bulkhead channel. The diaphragms seal onto wide rubber flaps riveted to the top of the mud shields, which often tear and hang loose. Headlamp buckets and glasses, if any, are also rubber sealed and age can let water in. Side window and 'B'post seals should be in good condition as should the front, side and rear sealing of convertible tops, although these may not be totally water or draught proof in the worst weather. The horizontal door glass felt and rubber wiper strips should be supple to prevent scratching the glass when raised or lowered.

Wheels and tyres

Check by tapping for loose spokes and look for corrosion. If possible, check spline condition (not Series 2 pressed steel wheels). Some Series 1 cars are fitted with the stronger forged 'smooth' hubs from series 2 cars rather than the original 'curly' shaped hubs. For the 'earless' spinners of S2 cars, check the removal tool comes with the car. Tyres of 185 original section on 5in rims give relaxed handling but look a little skinny in the wheel arches, so many run 6in rims and/or 205 or even 215 section tyres. If so, look for signs of rubbing at the rear bump stops.

Somebody paid good money to fit ugly tailpipes.

Exhaust

The 3.8 cars used 'long' chrome rear resonators, 4.2s a shorter pattern, which sprouted splayed rear outlets to clear the numberplate on S2 cars. The pipes connecting these to the central silencers are flattened where they pass under the rear suspension cage, but are often flattened further by ground contact, hurting performance. The silencer hangers vary between short and long wheelbase cars and the downpipes ahead of them are siamesed on 2+2s to avoid the optional automatic transmission. The manifolds should be shiny porcelain coated but this often cracks. Six-branch extractor exhausts can spoil low speed torque, unless carefully matched to other changes, and certainly generate more under-bonnet heat – especially long branch versions. On lefthand drive cars, the upper heat shields around the brake components must be present, as should the underfloor heat shields for all models.

Glass and wipers

<table>
<tr><td>Ex</td><td>Gd</td><td>Av</td><td>Po</td></tr>
<tr><td>4</td><td>3</td><td>2</td><td>1</td></tr>
</table>

Glass should be scratch-free with no milky delaminating areas. Sundym tint is acceptable and some had a heated rear window, with either a fine mesh aircraft type element, or the more obvious strip element of today's cars. The wires often break where they join the glass, although this can be repaired with care. The wipers should park on the driver's side along the lower edge of the glass, not several inches up. A common telltale for a US re-import car is wipers which still park on the left, though the car is now righthand drive. The parking can be altered easily on S1 cars but S1.5 and S2 cars use different motors and park mechanisms. Check the park adjustment knob and cable, which emerge from the S1 bulkhead, are not seized. Check for corrosion around wiper pivots and washers – although the washers moved to the bonnet on the 2+2 S2 cars, which have a more sloping screen to the front edge of the scuttle. Contrary to popular opinion, the Series 1 (and S1.5) 2+2 cars did not have a steeper windscreen angle – it merely looks that way, due to being about 1.5in higher at the top to match the raised roofline.

Telltale filler and corrosion around this S1.5 wiper pivot.

Rear suspension & brakes

<table>
<tr><td>Ex</td><td>Gd</td><td>Av</td><td>Po</td></tr>
<tr><td>4</td><td>3</td><td>2</td><td>1</td></tr>
</table>

Take off the wheels and jack the car by the correct bodywork jacking points to leave the rear suspension cage hanging. Look for rear cage mount separation, where the rubber sandwich meets the metal bracket. Refit the wheels, and check wheel bearings by rocking the wheel between 3 and 9 o'clock, watching that any play does not come from the hub carrier pivot bearings. Rock the wheel between 12 and 6 o'clock to feel for play in the differential output shaft bearings and the universal joints, which act as both driveshaft and suspension links. Rotating the wheel will check for clicking or grinding noises from the same areas.

The dampers and differential should be free of oil leaks and although a slight whine is acceptable, serious noise is not. Strange creaking from the rear on tight, slow turns probably just means the limited slip clutch is working, and is nothing to worry about. The handbrake cable, compensator mechanism and calipers often seize and should work freely, with no oil on the rear discs, which themselves should be largely corrosion free and without ridges. Check the flexible hose connecting the cage brake union to the long brake pipe under the body is sound, along with the pipe itself.

It is difficult to check for play at the inner and outer fulcrum pivots, but a tyre lever and some judicious prying will reveal serious wear. Fresh grease on all nipples and signs of spattering on adjacent bodywork bode well. The radius arm pivot bushes should be healthy-looking and the radius arm front fixing must be sound and free of slitting rubber or corroded bodywork. The anti-roll bar pivot rubbers and drop-link bushes must also be sound and not split or softened.

Front suspension, brakes & steering

Ex   Gd   Av   Po
4   3   2   1

Check the condition of all ball joints and look for split gaiters. Check the wheel bearings for play by rocking the raised wheel between 12 and 6 o'clock. The wishbone pivot and anti-roll bar rubbers should be clean and dry, not swollen or perished. From about early 1965, brake shields were fitted, but these have often been discarded – to the detriment of wet weather initial braking.

The steering should have minimal or no mechanical play at the rack bushes or track rod ends, and check also the universal joints at each end of the steering shaft – the lower one in particular can become dry and corroded, leading to significant play and stiffness at the same time. Pay special attention to the rubber rack mounts

securing the rack to the picture frame. These must be fitted with one extended safety bolt and spacers/penny washers on each side, to preserve control in the unlikely event of a mount delaminating. Feel for play in the steering wheel pivot, especially on the 3.8 cars, as the bushes were little more than compressed felt. The original wooden steering wheel has often delaminated and is a safety hazard if seriously split. New rims are available, as are complete wheels, at a price.

Steering rack mount with correct spacer and penny washer. Two are used here for extra security.

Look for corrosion on original Dunlop calipers and crosspipes, but don't assume the 3-pot Girling calipers used on S1.5/S2 cars are much better. Braided stainless steel Teflon-lined hoses look slightly out of place but are certainly beneficial in performance/feel terms. However, a standard E-type brake system in good condition is capable of overwhelming even modern tyres, so upgrades are not mandatory. The brake reservoirs should have small filters in the outlets and fluid should be fresh and clean, with no seepage from the rubber hoses or any other joint. The Reservac tank on the right footwell should be clean and corrosion-free, and sound hollow when tapped. It may fill with brake fluid if the servo is faulty. During any road test, check the brakes release properly, since faulty valves in the servo

Not all new parts are identical to the originals. This steering rack is good, but would lose points for originality.

cylinder or master cylinder can cause sticking, as can collapsed rubber hoses or corroded caliper pistons.

Some Series 1 cars were retro-fitted with power steering and many Series 2 cars, especially for North America, were fitted with a power steering system from the factory. Apart from checking hoses, unions, rack pipe-work and pump for leaks, there is not much that can be done beyond looking for a slack pump drive belt, and checking the condition and level of the reservoir fluid. Try operating the system from lock to lock when stationary, to check for odd noises or roughness, but provided the engine runs, the system will probably turn out to be in reasonable order.

Engine/gearbox mounts

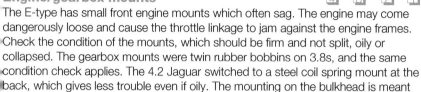

The E-type has small front engine mounts which often sag. The engine may come dangerously loose and cause the throttle linkage to jam against the engine frames. Check the condition of the mounts, which should be firm and not split, oily or collapsed. The gearbox mounts were twin rubber bobbins on 3.8s, and the same condition check applies. The 4.2 Jaguar switched to a steel coil spring mount at the back, which gives less trouble even if oily. The mounting on the bulkhead is meant to stabilize the engine, not take its full weight. If overtightened it can crack the bulkhead/firewall and will certainly transmit much noise and vibration to the cabin.

Cabin trim

Most 3.8 cars came with an aluminium dash and centre console trim, which is expensive and hard to replace in exactly the right pattern, so check its condition. Dash tops are an expensive moulded cover but are often bodged with vinyl, which is almost impossible to apply without leaving unsightly creases on this highly visible area. The 4.2 consoles are leather-covered instead of alloy, and the instrument panel on all models is black vinyl, which can occasionally split or bubble and come loose around the minor instruments. Of the Series 1 or 1.5 cars, only the 2+2 should have a lockable glove box lid and under-dash oddment shelves, although the lockable glove box became standard from Series 2 for all models. The glove box itself, and any under-dash shelves, are made of flock-lined cardboard and often collapse or distort, or lose their black lining to leave unsightly creases and 'bald' patches. All seat facings should be leather and the seat backs and sundry interior trim were velvet-like 'moquette' or vinyl, depending on the year.

Seats should slide easily and be plumply upholstered. The 4.2 seats have rubber diaphragms under the seat cushion, which must not be split or hanging loose. Alternative seat slider holes may be provided for taller drivers depending on the model, or may already be in use. Headrests on S2 cars can collapse because of foam degradation, but are repairable. Door cards often come loose or split due to water damage. Sun visors can split or get very limp, and the under-dash vinyl-trimmed alloy panels are often missing, leaving unsightly wiring in view. A full professional retrim kit for an E-type is expensive, so inspect the interior carefully.

Beautiful, spartan 3.8 cabin trim.

Telltale water traces on sill.
Not surprising since the
door seals are missing...

The headlining may be grubby but should be well-attached and complete, with good firm sun visors. At the back on FHC and 2+2 models, the plastic interior trim strip all around the rear hatch opening is often missing. Although not cheap, it is at least available again. The hatch should be supported by a locking brace or moveable prop, and if there is a heated rear glass, the wires should be intact and not pulled away from the base of the glass where they emerge through the rubber seal. The hatch body seal is often wrongly assembled.

Check the escutcheon springs are present around Series 1 door handles and window winders, to prevent them rattling against the doors. The two sections of door trim should be separated and held by upper chrome trim strips, again often missing or bodged. Not all models had armrests, but they should be sound if fitted. Apart from the earliest 3.8 FHC cars and from about 1965, the rear hatch hinges and latch should be protected by cup-shaped trim shields, with chrome beading around the edges and over the fixing flanges. These chrome edgings are often all or partially missing. On a convertible, check the condition of the outside corner of each seat back, as this can suffer damage from catching the soft top.

Carpets & luggage compartment

Ex [4] Gd [3] Av [2] Po [1]

All E-types were carpeted and had underfelt and sound-deadening anti-drum material fitted underneath. Carpets are held by special fasteners but often just curl up at the corners. A new set of carpets can hide terrible floor condition, so don't be fooled. High-wear areas are vinyl or rubber covered. Other areas of the lower interior are vinyl covered (inner sills, boot boards on FHC/2+2) or trimmed in 'Hardura' – a kind of vinyl/fibre trim panel that wipes clean and is flexible, but retains enough shape to trim vertical and complex shapes. Boot boards should be solid, and fitted with chrome and rubber protective strips. Early fixed head cars had a soft folding cover over the spare wheel rather than hard boards, but similar rubbing strips were used. Convertible models fitted with boot boards used a plain black painted wooden pattern, and all convertible cars, with or without boards, have the spare wheel area and sides of the boot covered with beige/'biscuit' loose Hardura trim, irrespective of body colour. Lift the boards or trim covers on all cars, and remove the spare wheel to check the boot floor for signs of poor welding repairs or crash wrinkles. A set of tools should be present, along with a jack.

Instruments & fuses

Ex [4] Gd [3] Av [2] Po [1]

All E-types came with at least six instruments plus an electric clock – fitted in the rev counter on S1 cars. The small clock often fails but can be repaired with modern electrics, as can the larger central clock used on S1.5 and S2 cars. The water and fuel gauges are controlled by a voltage stabiliser fixed to the back of the centre dash panel, so if both read low, this may be the cause. Series 2 cars replaced the ammeter with a voltmeter, which makes more sense for all the alternator-equipped 4.2 cars and is a useful swap for Series 1 4.2s. The rev counter on a 3.8 is redlined at 5500rpm, and for a 4.2 at 5000rpm. The speedo is matched to the differential ratio, and can read slow if the rear end has been changed from a low-geared North American ratio to the more long-legged European spec. Check all switches and gauges work and are not misted up or cracked. Undo the two thumbscrews at the top of the instrument panel and ease it gently forward, taking care not to break the switch legend strip on the lower console on S1 cars, and examine the general condition of the wiring and fuse panels.

Drop the dash panel to see what lies behind. This looks in good order.

Cooling system

The steel header tank often corrodes if antifreeze is neglected. Check for pitting and leaks, including at the Otter thermostatic switch which can give trouble when old or dirty. Hoses should be sound and show no corrosion around the alloy spigots onto which the upper ones fasten. The alloy radiator of 3.8 cars has often failed by now, and the brass 4.2 radiators have also often been replaced by modern copies in brass or alloy. The original single blade electric fan can struggle on S1 cars in hot weather, so the twin multi-blade S2 fans are generally better, but perhaps best of all is an upgrade such as the CoolCat fan motor with a modern fan blade. Kenlowe aftermarket fans are also good, although pricey, and they draw heavy current. Try to see if the modern fan upgrade has been fitted to mask a more fundamental problem, such as a silted-up block. Is the coolant clean and fresh-looking? Does the drain tap fitted to the left rear of the block work and run free? (It's best to ask the owner to demonstrate, rather than break something here.) Some S2 cars have a hexagonal block drain plug rather than a tap. Is the water pump free of play, and the belt and tensioner in good condition? If the spring-loaded tensioner is missing, this need not be an issue, provided a suitable size and type of belt has been fitted to permit adjustment by altering alternator/dynamo position as on other cars.

Aftermarket period header tank in brass. Quality varies but this should not corrode.

Fuel system

All six cylinder UK cars had triple SU 2in carburettors with a large triangular plenum (smooth on early 3.8s, triple ribbed on others) and a twin-horn filter canister. Any other filtration system is second-best, although if Webers or Dellortos are fitted, some kind of foam filter will probably be used. Most export market cars also had triple SUs – except for North America where, beginning with some of the S1.5 cars around 1967-1968, twin Strombergs were used with a modified manifold and plenum. Various types of cross-over, charge-warming, and secondary manifold systems were used – initially at the back of the engine and then over the centre of the cam boxes – but all robbed the car of performance in order to improve emissions. Late Series 2 cars used a pressed steel air filter with a modern style corrugated hose crossover, to draw warm air from over the shielded exhaust manifolds during warm-up.

SU float bowls should have narrow copper drains running down to a clip above the oil filter, but many have snapped off so that water finds its way into the carbs. The manual choke mechanism should be free and smooth, and clearly move the jets and set the fast idle. The float bowls should have small conical filters at their inlets, but this cannot usually be checked during inspection. Check that all three carbs and bowls look identical because some triple carb sets have been concocted from two XJ6 carbs and an odd carb from elsewhere. Check there are no obvious missing or mangled screws, and that the throttle linkage on the bulkhead works smoothly over the full range. The correct solid three-branch fuel supply pipe is expensive, and although it is possible to construct a neat system using individual banjos and flexible pipe, beware of any obvious bodges.

The single fuel filter is sometimes augmented by an in-line filter, in the line from the tank in the spare wheel well to protect the pump. If the car does not pull well under load on a road test it is possible that the filter is blocked, even if the float bowl appears clean, if one of the modern pleated gauze filters has been installed. This is because these pattern parts have fuel entering in the centre, and filtered fuel passing through the gauze into the fuel bowl, and then to the carbs. Since the dirt therefore collects out of sight inside the element (unlike the original filter design where the dirt stayed visible in the glass bowl), it is possible to think the filter is clear, when in fact it is full of rubbish when removed for inspection. On the right side of the spare wheel well is the fuel pump on 4.2 cars, whereas it is inside the tank on 3.8s. Check the lines are sound and dry, and that the wiring to the fuel sender is not frayed or broken. If possible, while the rear wheels are off for suspension inspection, feel for the fuel pipe where it emerges from the boot and runs along the chassis rail over the suspension. Being difficult to reach, this section of line is often neglected and the pipe may be seriously corroded. The engine should need some choke to start from cold but not normally from hot.

Cylinder head

Ex Gd Av Po
4   3   2   1

All Series 1 E-types, except possibly the very last ones, should have a gold coloured cylinder head, with a deeper pumpkin colour reserved for very early 3.8s. The front of the head around the breather tower should be smooth, not rough cast, except on later cars or cars fitted with engines from an XJ6, for example. The smooth cam covers are similarly satin polished and have chromed acorn nuts over thin copper washers, with the same style of nut used for cylinder head nuts over chromed D-shaped washers on most studs. Check the hidden nuts under the sides of the cam chain tower are present and the studs not stripped or missing. On Series 1 cars, the engine number is stamped at the back of the cam chain housing at the front of the valley. Series 2 cars dropped the gold colour and used silver painted and unnumbered heads with ribbed cam covers. The very first pattern had uninterrupted ribs and the word Jaguar cast in bas-relief, which is more attractive than the later versions, which had ribbing with gaps for the crossover pipework and a blank section onto which cheap Jaguar stickers were placed.

There should be a fibre conduit for the plug wires, and normally Champion 'bow tie' hard Bakelite plug caps, with some cars featuring rubber tubing, protecting the plug leads from the distributor over into the head valley. At the back of the inlet camshaft on S1 cars, there should be a small AC generator to power the tachometer, which is often temperamental. If the wires appear intact but the rev counter does not work, the tach generator is probably at fault.

Whilst at the back of the head, look to see there are no major oil leaks from the camshaft oil pipe banjos or split pipes, or coolant leaks from the plate or core plug at the back. Also look at the rear engine stabilizer rubber to see it is not split or soaked in oil, and that the bulkhead appears sound in this area.

Cylinder block

Ex 4 Gd 3 Av 2 Po 1

Check core plugs/freeze plugs for weeping or worse. The domed 3.8 types seem less reliable than the flanged press-in 4.2 types, but major problems are rare. Freezing or overheating can also cause typical cracking along the top of the block parallel to the face, near the middle cylinders, just below the head gasket level. Therefore, look carefully with a torch and mirror for any signs of mineral deposits or other leaking/cracking in this area. Blocks can be metal-stitched, but it means major surgery. The engine number is normally stamped above the oil filter housing but this changed to the left bell housing flange around the time of the Series 2 cars.

Oil leaks and pressure

Ex 4 Gd 3 Av 2 Po 1

Few E-types are completely dry underneath, but constant dripping indicates a problem. The rear cam feed connections can leak, as may the filter canister. More troublesome are the front gearbox seal or rear crank seal, especially if the car has not run for some time. If in doubt as to which one is the culprit, it may be possible to smell the oil on your fingertip for clues, as transmission oil has a distinct aroma, even if both appear black. Repairing either seal is an engine-out job. The cam covers should seal properly and the breather be clear all the way to the air cleaner. The oil return pipe to the sump from the filter block weeps sometimes, but is relatively easy to fix at oil change time by using the correct stepped hose or sleeving one end.

A cracked sump or stripped drain plug (all too common) will require more effort to repair. There should be no leaks from the front crank seal, the timing chest or breather housing. The gearbox and differential will last a long time with oil drips, provided the levels are kept topped up and oil does not reach the rear discs. Oil pressure when cold may reach 60-70psi or even higher briefly, but should settle to around 40psi when warm and running at 2000-3000rpm. However, oil senders are notoriously inaccurate, and the gauge reading may also be affected by voltage stabilizer gremlins. So unless a mechanical gauge is fitted, treat any given reading with a little scepticism, pending verification with a mechanical gauge. Confirmed low oil pressure may indicate little more than a stuck pressure relief valve, but when buying a car, it is wise to assume at least a strip and inspection of the engine bearings will be required to rule out worn mains or big ends. Some cars may have aftermarket spin-on filter adapters, or the Series 3 XJ6 filter block, though this requires some re-jigging of the bypass return pipe and the cam oil feeds.

Engine noise

Brief light rattling on start up from cold is acceptable, as is a constant rustle from the cam covers. Serious clatter from deep in the block, or the timing chest or cylinder head, spells trouble with pistons, timing chains or valve gear respectively – perhaps a loose tappet guide which will need urgent repair. Look inside the oil filler cap to see if screws or plates have been fitted to clamp the tappet guides in place. Audible pinging/pinking under load on road test is a bad sign, and may not easily be remediable by retarding the timing, if it is due to unsuitably high compression for the local fuel available. The cylinder head or block may have been skimmed to the point where a thicker head gasket is required to restore normal compression. The gearbox should be fairly silent in neutral, but the 3.8 Moss box will make a whine in first, as may most other boxes, especially if the reverse gear components were not de-burred during any rebuild.

Distributor and ignition

The distributor bob-weights should be free, and snap back under spring tension when released. There have been some recent reports of aftermarket rotor arms failing, although this may be partly due to fitting high power coils with or without electronic ignition. Some E-types, but not all, used vacuum timing adjustment (retard or advance). At inspection time it is probably enough to check that any lines on the distributor mate up with suitable lines on the carbs or manifold and no air leaks to either. The 3.8 cars used the screw-in spark plug leads, which are fiddly to make up properly, but secure when installed. Later cars used normal push-in leads. All versions benefit from small waterproofing sleeves over the cap connections. Points and condensers are so cheap, their condition is immaterial if the car at least runs. Electronic conversions, such as the Pertronix module, are popular – some owners have even fitted the entire Series 3 XJ6 distributor and amplifier from 79-86 cars, which uses a cheap GM AC/Delco ignition module. If a car fails to start but has been worked on, it may be worthwhile checking the distributor was not placed 180 degrees out of phase. The rotor arm should be pointing at the lead going to the front cylinder (No 6 in Jaguar parlance) when that cylinder is at or near TDC on the compression stroke, as verified by turning the engine with that plug removed.

The Lucas coil is normally mounted in front of the head, behind the expansion tank on Series 1 cars, but moved to one of several positions alongside the engine on Series 2 cars, depending on date and whether air conditioning or power steering, etc, were fitted, which required significant shuffling of under-bonnet ancillary locations. All Series 1 cars used a normal 12V coil originally, powered from the negative side on 3.8s and the positive side on negative earth 4.2 cars.

Some Series 2 cars used a ballast resistor system and lower voltage coil, but many have been converted back to normal 12V operation, and one or two Series 1 cars are accidentally or purposely running ballast coils and resistors. Provided the coil voltage matches the use or absence of a resistor, there is not much to choose between them, although many feel that the simplest system is always the best and so drop the resistor and choose a full 12V coil.

Clutch and pedal assemblies

Ex Gd Av Po 4 3 2 1

The clutch is heavy but not unduly so, and should release completely every time. Being an hydraulic system, the seals in the master or slave cylinder can leak, so check for fluid on the carpet or along the lines and bellhousing. The clutch, brake and throttle each have return springs of different patterns but these are often broken, so check for lazy or sloppy actions. The organ pedal accelerator on LHD cars is often bent in the middle. Pedal pads can be adjusted up or down along the levers to some extent, and levers can be adjusted forward or backwards by means of stop screws on some cars, but be sure there is always some free play at the pedal and also at the slave cylinder on the bell housing.

Electrical

Ex Gd Av Po 4 3 2 1

The 3.8 cars used a positive-earth dynamo system, whereas 4.2 cars switched to a negative-earth alternator system, which is better in traffic at least, and more like today's cars, in that it achieves full charge current at lower rpm and can sustain greater overall electrical loads. Check the overall wiring for tidiness and splits/bare connections, etc. Trouble spots include dirty relays for the horn mounted on the left wheel arch mud shield and sometimes, but not always, a relay fitted for the thermostatic fan switch. The switch itself often fails, although originals can be cleaned. A solid-state modern switch is a good, though minor, selling point. Cars may suffer poor charging control due to old or failed components, damaged wiring, malfunctioning switches and corroded fuses and holders. Most faults are due to age or corrosion, and can be rectified with careful dismantling and cleaning. From about 1965, there should be protective shields usually both above and behind the alternator, to keep exhaust heat away, but these are often missing. Apart from looking for evidence of botching and checking for any electrical items which do not work, there is not too much else the lay person can do to inspect things during a simple pre-sale review.

Graham Heritage's 66 shows no sign of clutch trouble. Check for leaks and free play.

The horns, brackets and connections often corrode, and in some markets (such as the UK) if only the high or low tone work, as opposed to both, it is an MoT inspection failure point. Series 1 cars used the centre horn push on the steering wheel and as this mechanism involves a rather fiddly series of wiper contacts and insulators, etc, it is worth verifying that all works as it should. Series 2 cars use a simpler horn push on the end of the indicator stalk, but even here the wires can fray or break where they emerge from the stalk into the switch body itself. Indicator/turn signal switches are once more available new from suppliers such as SNG Barratt, but the small scale remanufacture means they are inevitably quite expensive, so check everything works. One type uses a plastic spring which is available separately but other versions are more complex. In all cases, check the self-cancelling function works by turning the steering wheel. This is a common failure point once the nylon self-cancelling ring becomes brittle after four decades.

Starting with the 1966 introduction of the 2+2 model in North American markets, a system of hazard warning flashers was fitted gradually to all cars. The first version was a fairly crude 'add-on' bracket, housing a switch, a warning lamp and a label below the left dashboard panel. This later gained a small plastic cover to hide the wiring and auxiliary flasher unit, eventually being properly integrated into the car's electrical system on Series 1.5 cars and subsequent, which used rocker switches instead of toggles. Both types of switch, incidentally, can be rebuilt at home with care and delicate tools.

The headlamps are not great at the best of times on Series 1 cars, partly due to light loss through the glass covers and partly due to shadows thrown because of the bonnet recesses. Series 1 lamp buckets are exposed to heavy stone chipping and may corrode badly, and the wires chafe. All frontal lighting and horn power is fed through a single large multi-pin connector, and this too can corrode and is expensive to replace, leading to some using cheap trailer-type connectors which do not fit properly.

The harness from the main frame to the bonnet is a long plastic-sleeved extension, and careless routing around the frame and bonnet hinge area can lead to chafing or stretching, with inevitable damage that is tricky to fix due to poor access and an often dirty environment. Check all the lights work, front and rear, and if there are mysterious stray flashings or dimming as you work through the side light, main light and indicator switches, this is often due to poor earth connections rather than major trouble. Earthing/grounding problems can be infuriating to track down but at least do not take much money to fix.

The heater fan is not the most efficient compared to modern systems, but was at least a standard fitment and a two-speed design, unlike many of its contemporaries. A cheap and effective replacement for a rusted-out or damaged original is a generic motor, available for very few dollars from Grainger's electrical wholesalers in the USA. The original motors can be dissected and new brushes or bearings made and fitted, but it is usually not worth the effort. There should be a wire-wound resistor mounted under the heater box to provide the two-speed operation, but the tabs may be snapped or missing altogether.

Wiper motors are available but expensive, although the rare three-wire 'hybrid' type with self-contained parking mechanism, used on Series 1.5 cars for a year, is harder to find. Check wipers operate at two speeds and park properly on the driver's side. Wipers which park on the passenger side are a sign of a car with converted steering.

Washer equipment was a sturdy glass bottle Rolls-Royce/Aston Martin type on 3.8s, which changed to a smaller, lighter, white plastic bottle on 4.2 cars. The motors may have worn out long ago and were not up to today's standards when they were new, but should at least function. Do check this, and if the motor appears to work but nothing emerges from the washer jets on Series 1 cars or Series 2 convertible/FHC (not 2+2) beware of disconnected piping inside the bulkhead. Stray screen fluid can lead to serious internal corrosion if not spotted quickly. Series 2 2+2 cars and all series 3 E-types (see separate V12 E-type book) used a single twin-jet washer mounted on the bonnet rather than the bulkhead/firewall.

Air conditioned cars obviously have extra wiring and motors, compressors, condensers, etc, and these varied according to whether the system was factory fitted or dealer fitted. Apart from the use of non-CFC gas nowadays, simple air conditioning systems have not changed a great deal and if you decide to retain any such parts, they can normally be checked/repaired by specialists without too much trouble.

Evaluation procedure

Add up the total points scored.
128 points = first class, possibly concours;
90 points = good/very good;
65 points = average;
32 points = poor.
Cars scoring over 90 should be completely usable and require the minimum of repair, although continued maintenance and care will be required to keep them in condition. Cars scoring between 32 and 65 points will require a full restoration – the cost of which will be much the same regardless of points scored. Cars scoring between 66 and 89 points will require very careful assessment of the necessary repair/restoration costs in order to arrive at a realistic purchase value.

Current inspection certificates don't ensure a great car.

10 Auctions
– Sold! Another way to buy your dream

Auction pros & cons

Pros: Auctions are where dealers buy and sell, so they operate as trade rather than retail markets. This means that except for the so-called 'Prestige' auctions, prices are often lower than those on dealer premises and of some private sellers, so you could grab a bargain on the day. Auctioneers have usually confirmed ownership title with the seller and at the venue it should be possible to check this and any other relevant paperwork. You may also receive 24 hours warranty cover.

Cons: You can normally only get either minimal information before travelling to the venue, or vague and sometimes very sales-orientated descriptions. Learn to read between the lines and only visit if there are several candidate cars, to avoid disappointment if the single one of interest is withdrawn early or sold elsewhere. Star lots may be stored indoors under good light, but even so, there is limited scope to examine the cars thoroughly. The wise buyer gets to the venue early and you'll do well to bring this book, a mirror and torch. Classic cars are normally not started and cannot be road tested, so for nearby venues try to arrive early on preview days to see the lots arriving and being off-loaded or marshalled into position. Being trade sales, the cars often need valeting, which dealers are happy to do and should not put you off.

Do your research, decide your personal limit and stick to it. Don't forget to budget for the auctioneer's charges to buyers as well as sellers, or you may get a shock at the extra 5-10%. Admission is normally paid for by catalogue and usually covers two people, so take a friend as it's amazing what a second pair of eyes can spot.

Catalogue prices and payment details

Auction catalogues normally feature an estimated price and will spell out all charges and acceptable payment methods. Be sure you can comply before bidding. An immediate part-payment or deposit is usually requested if you win, with the balance payable within 24 hours. Check for cash and credit card limits, if any, and options such as personal cheques/checks and debit cards or banker's drafts. The car won't be released until all costs are cleared, with storage normally at your expense until the process is completed.

Viewing

In some instances, it's possible to view the day before as well as hours before an auction. Staff or owners may unlock doors, engine and luggage compartments for inspection or even start the engine on request. Crawling around the car is fine but you may not jack up a vehicle – hence your torch and mirror on a stick. It is often possible to view documents associated with the vehicle too.

Bidding

Lots are sold in numerical order, so get to the sale room in good time and gauge the activity and the auctioneer's quirks. Phrases such as 'It's with me at ...' mean the car has not yet reached reserve, whereas 'It's for sale at ...' means the car will now go to the highest bidder.

Make sure the auctioneer gives you eye contact at each bid until you make it clear you have withdrawn, by looking away and shaking your head.

Unsold cars may still be open to offers via the auctioneers. Such bids, if successful, are often announced to the room shortly afterwards to keep the momentum going.

If you win

You need to decide how you will get the car home, immediately or after final payment completion. Insurance, or a trailer to collect the vehicle will be needed. Auctioneers will normally give details of specialists who will be happy to deliver the car, for a price.

eBay & the internet

eBay and other online auctions cover the best and the worst of the auction spectrum. It may be possible to bid across continents yet have a trusted person inspect the car in person and report back to you. Owner's clubs and groups such as jag-lovers.org are ideal for this, although you should offer payment for their time or expenses and decide that you will trust their advice.

Most on-line sources show the seller's location, and may even allow you to search by given distances from your home, which can be useful. Always check, however, that the car is actually at the seller's location. It is usually best to choose your upper limit and bid that at the outset.

Remember, that a winning bid is binding and that it will be very difficult to obtain satisfaction if a dishonest seller disappears with your money, or a car never arrives because it never existed. You have been warned ...

Auctioneers

Barrett-Jackson www.barrett-jackson.com/ Bonhams www.bonhams.com/ British Car Auctions (BCA) www.bca-europe.com or www.british-car-auctions. co.uk/ Cheffins www.cheffins.co.uk/ Christies www.christies.com/ Coys www. coys.co.uk/ eBay www.ebay.com or www.ebay.co.uk/ H&H www.classic-auctions.co.uk/ RM www.rmauctions.com/ Shannons www.shannons.com.au/ Silver www.silverauctions.com.

11 Paperwork
– correct documentation is essential!

The paper trail

E-types often come with a large document file accumulated by a succession of proud owners. Cars imported from their original market tend to have less information, so uncovering their history is often difficult. Documentation represents the true history of the car, showing the level of use and care it has received, which specialists have worked on it and the dates of major repairs and restorations. This information will be extremely valuable to you, so be very sceptical of cars supposedly having undergone extensive work for which there is no confirmatory paperwork.

Registration documents

All countries/states have some form of registration for private vehicles whether its like the American 'pink slip' system or the British 'log book' system.

It is essential to check that the registration document is genuine, that it relates to the car in question, and that all the vehicle's details are correctly recorded, including chassis/VIN and engine numbers (if these are shown). If you are buying from the previous owner, his or her name and address will be recorded in the document: this will not be the case if you are buying from a dealer.

In the UK the current (Euro-aligned) registration document is named 'V5C,' and is printed in coloured sections of blue, green and pink. The blue section relates to the car specification, the green section has details of the new owner and the pink section is sent to the DVLA in the UK when the car is sold. A small section in yellow deals with selling the car within the motor trade.

Previous ownership records

Due to important new legislation on data protection, it's no longer possible to acquire, from the British DVLA, a list of previous owners of a car. This scenario will also apply to dealerships and other specialists, from who you may wish to make contact and acquire information on previous ownership and work carried out.

If the car has a foreign registration, there may be expensive and time-consuming formalities to complete. Do you really want the hassle?

Roadworthiness certificate

Most administrations require that vehicles are regularly tested to prove they are safe to use on the public highway and don't produce excessive emissions. They are usually carried out at approved testing stations and any available old certificates may show the mileage and location at those dates, confirming the car's history. If the car is not roadworthy it should be moved by trailer but ideally a car will be on the road, tested and/or licensed as necessary, which should permit a test drive with, or by the owner.

Road licence

In the UK, if a car is untaxed because it has not been used for some time, the owner has to complete a Statutory Off Road Notification (SORN) to inform the licensing authorities. Failure to do so will create an automatic fine and the vehicle's date-related registration number may be lost, resulting in lots of aggravation to get it re-registered. This does not yet apply to cars which were already off the road long before that legislation came into effect. On the plus side, in the UK at least, all 6-cylinder E-types were built before the end of 1972 and are therefore exempt from paying road tax, although formalities still need to be completed. Similar age-related exemptions apply in other countries for which the E-type may be eligible.

Certificates of authenticity

The Jaguar Daimler Heritage Trust (www.jdht.com) is sponsored by Jaguar. It provides Production Record Trace Certificates for a small fee to those who can prove ownership and supply the four key serial numbers (chassis, body, engine and gearbox), all of which are shown on the car's ID plate. The certificate confirms if those numbers belong together and will detail the despatch date, model type, original interior and exterior colours, original distributor and sometimes the first owner and registration number.

If the car has been used in European classic car rallies, it may have a FIVA (Federation International des Vehicules Anciens) certificate. The so-called 'FIVA Passport,' or 'FIVA Vehicle Identity Card,' enables organisers and participants to recognise whether or not a particular vehicle is suitable for individual events. If you want to obtain such a certificate go to www.fbhvc.co.uk or www.fiva.org. There will be similar organisations in other countries too.

Valuation certificate

Hopefully, the vendor will have a recent valuation certificate, or letter signed by a recognised expert stating how much he, or she, believes the particular car to be worth (such documents, together with photos, are usually needed to get 'agreed value' insurance). Generally, such documents should act only as confirmation of your own assessment of the car, rather than a guarantee of value, because the expert has probably not seen the car in person. See chapter 16 for organisations able to provide formal valuations. Sellers who insist on achieving sale prices matching these valuations exactly are not being realistic.

Service & restoration history

If the car has been restored, expect receipts and photographs or other evidence from a specialist restorer. Pictures taken at various stages and from various angles should help you gauge the thoroughness of the work and if they are for the same car. Make it a condition of purchase that you receive at least copies of such photographs, if not the originals.

Items like the original bill of sale, handbook, parts invoices and repair or parts bills all add to the story and character of the car. Even a correct brochure for the car's model year, or original contemporary road tests are useful documents that might take a lot of finding in future. In the likely absence of service paperwork, your assessment of the car's overall condition is the best guide.

12 What's it worth to you?
– let your head rule your heart!

Condition

Negotiate on the basis of your condition assessment (chapter 9) and for a supposed usable car, offer your estimates for any fault rectification you consider necessary, but be realistic if the car is being sold honestly with acknowledged failings. Classic magazine price guides, where available, are the best way of finding up-to-date estimates of value for your specific model in local currency. You may need to adapt your estimate of condition to the system used by the magazine but this should not be too difficult.

You can also show relevant auction values, or eBay prices (which are often low) to support your offer. Most guides show prices for dealer sales and private sales but, before you start haggling with the seller, consider what effect any variation from standard specification might have on the car's value (see below).

Desirable options/extras

Coopercraft 4-pot brakes peep out from behind a 3.8 front wheel. Volvo conversions are far cheaper, but require extra work.

The Kenlowe fan is clumsy but effective. The K&N filters are non-original.

For some, anything non-standard reduces the value of the car. For people who like to use their cars, deviations from standard may not be just acceptable, but positively desirable.

E-types were sold with silver-painted wire wheels as standard and chrome was extra, but almost every US car had chrome wheels. Most buyers prefer wire wheels on Series 2 cars, many of which originally came with pressed steel wheels.

Series 2 wire wheels have smooth hubs that are easier to clean and are stronger forgings than the pressed steel 'curly hub' design used on Series 1 cars. Modern wheels such as Dayton or MWS, with stainless spokes and sealed spoke heads to permit tubeless tyres, are better than standard wheels, unless total originality is the aim.

Original size 5in rims make for an easy-driving car with progressive and controllable handling on the limit. Modern 6in or wider rims offer more ultimate grip and fill the wheel arches better, at the cost of snappier breakaway when the limits of adhesion are reached at higher speeds. Alloy wheels of the Minilite or D-type pattern look good on E-types, especially if they retain the splined attachment, or in the case of the D-type pattern, a works-type peg-drive system.

Triple SU carburettors and standard air filtration are valuable and effective upgrades to US-market S2 E-types. Brake upgrades, such as modern 4-pot calipers, work well, especially on 3.8l cars which also benefit from conversion to a 4.2 type servo, but there is little wrong with good stock brakes. S2 front suspension uprights and three-pot calipers can be used on S1 cars. The larger S3 V12 servo is a useful upgrade to any 4.2 E-type.

For convertibles, a factory hard top is a valuable option but requires careful storage when not on the car.

Electronic ignition is one of the best and cheapest upgrades, with a modern electric fan and thermostatic switch close behind. A 5-speed gearbox is one of the most expensive upgrades but also worth having for a non-concours driver car, especially with low USA gearing, assuming the transmission tunnel has not been cut about. The 2+2s can accommodate a Jaguar 4-speed with overdrive, which gives many of the benefits of a 5-speed at a fraction of the cost. Fitting an all-synchro box to a 3.8 also improves driveability but is probably at best neutral to value, if not a little detrimental, due to being non-original except on the very last few 3.8s in 1964. A 3.8 flywheel is lighter than the 4.2's and makes the engine feel livelier, but be aware of going too light flywheel-wise on a road car.

Alloy radiators are good (most 3.8s came so equipped) but brass 4.2 equipment, in good condition, works well enough if the engine is not silted up and the thermostatic fan switch is

A battery isolator switch is fitted to this scruffy car. The engine breather is pointing straight at the brake caliper. Not a good idea!

Desirable locking fuel cap in a beautifully-finished filler area, apart from the missing bicycle tyre buffers.

working correctly. A solid state switch is generally more reliable and whatever the type of switch, a modern fan and motor is a definite upgrade because of the newer design, materials and the multi-blade fan design. CoolCat fans use the standard mounts and fan shroud, whereas some others like the Kenlowe, come with their own extra mounts and usually sit in front of the radiator and tend to use a lot of current (which may be problematic on a dynamo-equipped car in traffic). Suppliers such as Derek Watson can supply beautifully made alloy radiators and matched shrouded fans, but at a price reflecting the quality.

Triple SU retro-fit to an American S2. Love the improvised rubber seal strips!

Stainless exhausts can make the exhaust note sound a little 'tinny' but last well. E-type Fabrications make is probably the most beautiful tubular manifolds and exhausts on the market, yet surprisingly they are not the most expensive. Adjustable shock absorbers like the high-quality alloy-bodied Classic Jaguar brand in the USA are worth having. Gaz or Spax shocks are more easily available in Europe, and Konis are not

Solid-state Otter switch replacement. This version is from CoolCat Corp.

so much adjustable in the normal easy sense, as capable of being changed to one of three settings once removed and dismantled. Rob Beere in the UK, and several US vendors, offer adjustable reaction plates to simplify setting the front torsion bars. Bolt-type ones seem to be more user-friendly than the snail cam pattern.

Halogen lights and a mechanical oil pressure gauge are improvements over the originals, yet almost undetectable, as are a solid state instrument voltage regulator or charging regulator. Converting a positive-earth dynamo to negative earth may be worthwhile if you intend to do significant mileage, but is expensive. Changing to a modern alternator is cheaper and in many cases an improvement over a tired Lucas original. Volt meters are more useful than ammeters on 4.2 S1 cars.

An alloy bonnet or other panels are useful and expensive, but being softer metal they dent more easily.

Undesirable features

A car with non-matching numbers is always worth less, although the difference may be small. In practical terms, the replacement engine or gearbox may be just as good, or possibly 'better' than the original. For example, the later big-valve XJ6 engine is both stronger and faster than the E-type from 20 years earlier, but unless the original engine comes with the car, use of the XJ6 unit will hurt its value. Less clear-cut is the effect of fitting an improved all-synchro gearbox to a 3.8 (although the final 3.8s came with the all-synchro box as standard). Similarly, some buyers would pay a premium for a 5-speed in any E-type, but for the top-end concours cars the original type box, especially matching number, is most valuable.

On the left a new, stronger, engine mount: on the right a more typical, collapsed mount.

Opinion is divided on cars with a vinyl sunroof – some love them and some feel they ruin the car. They were certainly plentiful period accessories and do give a fresh air feel to a closed car. There is little debate over automatics, however. Despite selling very well in the USA, particularly when new, the slush-box 2+2 cars are almost universally disliked today. Conversion to the 4-speed synchro (with a rear extension for the 2+2) improves the value of the car but a converted automatic 'BW' suffix car will always be worth less than an original manual car. If you actually want an automatic, this bargaining point is to your advantage, since you will be in the minority and the seller will be glad to find someone prepared to take the car 'as is.' The same goes for LHD cars on sale in the UK needing conversion to RHD, or vice versa in LHD markets.

Power steering and air conditioning can help sell a car in the USA, where many S2 cars were equipped with these extras straight from the factory and a significant number of S1 cars were converted by dealers or private individuals. Far fewer were sold this way outside the USA, and the extra equipment is generally regarded as reducing value because it is just extra equipment to go wrong and it hurts the car's weight, performance and under-bonnet appearance.

Triple Weber carbs or Dellortos have eye-appeal but can lack effective air filtration, consume more fuel and can make the car less tractable unless set up perfectly. The same goes for performance camshafts, large bore exhausts and ultra-light flywheels. There is a market for tuned cars with all the above, but standard cars sell better. Fibreglass panels are light and don't rust but detract from any E-type's value, except those in race trim. Alloy panels are more valuable than fibreglass but dent more easily than steel, and except on a track car, would generally not add significant value over a standard car. A full alloy bonnet is a possible exception for some buyers. Obviously, any car fitted with a non-Jaguar engine or other major parts from other manufacturers is worth far less than an all-Jaguar car.

Check all suspension rubbers and joint covers are good, as here on Joe Hardy's lower ball joints.

Striking a deal

An E-type is only worth what someone is prepared to pay for it. If 'your' car has been on sale for some time, this might dawn on the seller and help you get the car for less than they're asking. Be prepared to walk away because there are plenty of E-types around, but don't miss striking a deal on a car you want for the sake of a few pounds, especially if it is local or has other attractive attributes.

A big-valve XJ6 engine is perfectly at home in an E-type.

13 Do you really want to restore?

– it'll take longer and cost more than you think

If you have appropriate skills and a little patience, you may be happy to purchase a car requiring moderate remedial work before being put back on the road. This kind of car is reasonably plentiful in both trade and private hands, but needs to be sifted carefully from cars looking superficially similar but requiring a total rebuild. Even if you are prepared to take on major work, and therefore include acknowledged poor condition cars in your search, you still need to be aware of the full extent of

Decide if you really want to have to deal with this sort of problem yourself.

the damage in order to avoid paying significant money for what turns out to be a largely worthless pile of rust and rubber.

Take care to think through the type of work you are equipped to do. Some people have the patience, tools and skills to restore bodywork but find mechanical or electrical work intimidating. Others will happily strip an XK engine to its tiniest components (and lose half of them) but steer clear of panel beating or spraying. Be realistic and recognise that it is easy to overreach yourself, especially if you

have a definite schedule in mind for when you want the car to be ready. There are lots of professionals around to help, but their clientele is usually well-heeled, and the best specialists are often booked up long in advance and can charge premium rates as a consequence. The rule should always be to buy the best car you can afford as the cheapest and quickest way to a good E-type experience.

If the restoration process itself is intended as your long-term hobby, and you can accept that the finished car is probably years away, then you can consider the lower end of the market as your entry point.

Rebuild projects and 'basket cases'

Taking on an E-type as your first car restoration is not usually a wise choice. If you have the requisite extensive skills and/or deep pockets, it is possible to restore or remanufacture almost anything, but E-types are a notorious moneypit and many uncompleted projects have been sold on halfway through restoration due to lack of funds, time, storage space, or all three. The cost of professionally restoring a basket case far outstrips the value of the finished car, so it usually makes more sense to buy a complete good vehicle and use it immediately, or perform a 'rolling restoration' and enjoy it during the summer whilst repairing a whining diff or doing a retrim, etc, during successive winters. Be prepared for reliability glitches until the car is completely refurbished.

DIY restoration of a poor E-type can be measured in decades or numbers of children born or house moves completed. Routinely, the boxes of bits are missing some elusive, expensive parts. If, however, as in the author's case, a dismantled car is your only realistic entry into the world of E-type ownership, be prepared for a long hard slog. At least buying a basket case normally allows you to examine parts, like picture frames, more closely for rust flakes inside, and wheels, exhausts and suspension, etc, for overall condition.

Would you really know enough to ensure you used these steering rack safety bolts? Even some so-called 'pro' shops forget them.

Beware of 'shipwright's disease,' whereby the more parts you refurbish, the more you come across other parts which are now comparatively substandard and you decide to refurbish or replace those as well. At least there is a thriving trade in secondhand spares but it is axiomatic that the time and financial cost of restoring a good car, let alone a basket case, is always higher than you first thought.

Could you honestly sort this out?

14 Paint problems
– bad complexion, including dimples, pimples and bubbles

Paint faults generally occur due to lack of protection or poor preparation during a respray or touch up. However, on an E-type of all cars, do **not** confuse a simple paint fault with what may be a symptom of rushed repairs over structural rust, or the first signs of such corrosion coming through from underneath. Remember also, given the inherent value of a good car, that it is worth spending more time and effort on an E-type's paintwork than might be justified with a mass-produced car of much lower potential value, even in concours condition.

Some of the following conditions may be present in the car you're looking at:

Orange peel
This appears as an uneven paint surface, similar to the dimpled skin of an orange. It is caused by failure of atomized paint droplets to flow into each other on the painted surface. It's sometimes possible to polish out the effect with paint cutting compound or very fine abrasive paper on a soft block. A respray may be necessary in severe cases. Consult a bodywork repairer/paint shop for advice. If the paint is 2 pack, it will be very hard to flatten.

Cracking
Severe cases are likely to have been caused by too heavy an application of paint (or filler beneath the paint). Also, insufficient stirring of the paint before application can lead to the components being improperly mixed, and cracking can result. Incompatibility with the paint already on the panel can have a similar effect. To rectify the problem, it is necessary to rub down to a smooth, sound finish before respraying the problem area. Resprayed E-types can suffer heat cracking near bonnet vents on the exhaust side, so take special care here.

Cracking from the red-hot lights? Bad paint more like.

Crazing
Sometimes the paint takes on a crazed rather than a cracked appearance, when the problems mentioned under 'Cracking' are present. This problem can also be caused by a reaction between the underlying surface and the paint. Paint removal and respraying the problem area is usually the only solution.

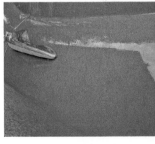

When does cracking become crazing? Presumably somebody paid good money fo this terrible paint job.

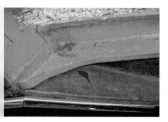

Recent paint is blistering. Sadly, it is probably a corrosion problem rather than a paint issue.

Blistering

Almost always caused by corrosion of the metal beneath the paint. Usually perforation will be found in the metal and the damage will almost always be far worse on an E-type than that suggested by the area of blistering, especially near the bulkhead/sill join or other lead-loaded areas. The metal will have to be repaired before repainting.

Micro blistering

Usually the result of an economy respray, where inadequate heating has allowed moisture to settle on the car before spraying. Consult a paint specialist, but usually damaged paint will have to be removed before partial or full respraying. It can also be caused by car covers that don't 'breathe.'

Fading

Some colours, especially reds, are prone to fading if subjected to strong sunlight for long periods, even with the benefit of polish protection. Sometimes proprietary paint restorers and/or paint cutting compounds will retrieve the situation but a respray may be the only real solution if you are unhappy about driving a car with 'patina.'

Peeling

Often a problem with metallic paintwork when the sealing lacquer becomes damaged and begins to peel off. Poorly applied paint may also peel. The remedy is to strip and start again!

Dimples

Dimples in the paintwork are caused by the residue of polish (particularly silicone types) not being removed properly before re-spraying. Paint removal and repainting is the only solution – localized if possible, extensive if necessary. Remember this problem was caused by insufficient care in the first place...

Dents

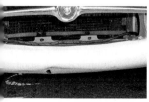

The hole is normal for a US license-plate tilt mechanism. The dents are not …

Small dents are usually easily cured by a 'Dentmaster' operative, or equivalent technician, who can pull or push out the dent (if the paint surface is still intact). Companies offering dent removal services usually come to your home: consult your telephone directory or ask at a local prestige car dealer for personal recommendation. Be aware that E-types are made of thicker steel with stronger compound curves than many flimsy modern cars, so the job may take them longer and cost more than anticipated.

15 Problems due to lack of use
– just like their owners, E-types need exercise!

Cars deteriorate slowest if exercised regularly. A run of at least ten miles, once a week, is recommended for classics. Beware of starting the engine and switching it off before totally hot, as this is worse than never running the car.

Seized components
S1 brakes are prone to problems because unlike modern calipers, the seal wipes the cast-iron cylinder surface rather than a moving piston. The master and servo cylinder(s) are more conventional but can corrode or fill with slime from old fluid or deteriorated rubber hose. The small piston in the nose of the 4.2 slave cylinder may become sluggish, making the brakes stick. The vacuum check valve on the Reservac tank can also fail through lack of use. Handbrake/emergency brake calipers, cables and especially the compensator mechanism are notorious for seizing, so pay special attention to lubricating such parts. The leather differential seals can also deteriorate on prolonged standing.

The clutch may seize if the plate becomes stuck to the flywheel because of corrosion or can refuse to engage if it sticks on corroded splines after pedal release. So regularly working through the gears and easing the clutch to and fro whilst the engine warms up is a must, if it is not practicable to take the car for a run because of the season.

Fluids
Old, acidic oil will corrode shaft bearings and polished or machined surfaces, as will 'fresh' oil repeatedly loaded with combustion and condensation products from briefly starting up a large cold XK engine. Check for a 'mayonnaise' appearance under the filler cap or dipstick. Old antifreeze or plain water will play havoc with E-type water passages, corrode and silt up the block and in extreme cases perforate the alloy water pump housing, letting coolant into the sump. Lack of antifreeze can cause core plugs to be pushed out or crack the block or head. Brake fluid absorbs water from the atmosphere and should be renewed every two years. Old fluid with a high water content causes corrosion, piston/caliper seizure and brake failure if the water turns to vapour near hot braking components.

Tyres
Tyres that take the weight of the car in a single position for long periods will develop flat spots. Tyre walls may crack or bulge. Tyres have an approximately 8-year shelf life depending on conditions, and regular use helps preserve them. Certainly do not risk poor tyres on a car as powerful as an E-type. Ask a local tyre specialist how to decipher your tyre's date codes, which may vary by region.

Shock absorbers (dampers)

With lack of use, the dampers can corrode on the piston rod. Creaking, groaning, stiff suspension and leaks are signs of this problem.

Rubber and plastic

Radiator hoses can perish and split, possibly resulting in loss of all coolant. Window and door seals can harden and leak. Steering, suspension gaiters and wiper blades will harden.

Electrics

The battery will be of little use if it has not been charged for many months. Earthing/ grounding problems are common when the connections have corroded. Old bullet and spade type electrical connectors corrode and may need disconnecting, cleaning and protection (eg Vaseline), and wire insulation can crack.

Exhaust

Exhaust fumes contain water and acids, so mild steel exhausts corrode from the inside when the car is not used, or is shut off before totally warmed up.

Unused engines can rust internally.

16 The Community
– key people, organisations and companies in the E-type world

Perhaps not surprisingly, given the emotions stirred by these evocative cars, there is a support network second to none for lovers of the Jaguar marque in general, and for the E-type in particular.

It is possible to go from knowing practically nothing to becoming very well-versed in a matter of weeks, if you absorb yourself in some of the literature and support resources that are available internationally and in most large markets. Thanks to the internet, it is even possible to put specific technical queries to a panel of experts on various bulletin boards and forums, and receive first-class advice in minutes or hours. Of course there is also unsound advice on offer, but it is generally not too hard to tell the difference, and most of the good resources are self-policing, so that bad advice is usually corrected fairly quickly.

Clubs

Jaguar Drivers' Club, 18 Stuart Street, Luton, Bedfordshire, LU1 2SL, England
Tel: +44 (0)1582 419332
www.jaguardriver.co.uk
One of the best established clubs, set up with factory support originally, and covering the full range from the earliest cars to today's models. It has a good web site, excellent magazine, specialist E-type section, insurance schemes and offers valuations, etc. Extensive overseas network.

Jaguar Enthusiasts' Club, Abbeywood Office Park, Emma Chris Way, Filton, Bristol, BS34 7JU, England
Tel: +44 (0)1179 698186
www.jec.org.uk
The world's largest Jaguar club, originally an offshoot of the Jaguar Driver's Club but now pre-eminent in the field, and offering the usual good magazine as well as tool hire services, specially commissioned spares remanufacture and events for every taste. Also very useful JagAds internet and print-based advertisement facility.

Jaguar E-type Club, PO Box 2, Tenbury Wells, Worcestershire, WR15 8XX, England
Tel: +44(0)1584 781588
www.e-typeclub.com
Phillip Porter's new club dedicated to the E-type alone. It is rather up-market, according to some ex-members, and perhaps formed with an eye to having a leading role when the E-type's 50th anniversary comes around? Philip Porter owns the famous 9600 HP Geneva launch car. If your only Jaguar interest is the E-type, then it's one to consider.

Jaguar Clubs of North America, 500 Westover Drive, No 8354, Sanford, NC 27330
Tel: +1 502 244 1672
www.jcna.com
It has a good web site, technical articles, US club network and events calendar. Superbly detailed and painstakingly-compiled concours originality guides for each series, which are probably the best source of information of correct original finishes for almost every part.

www.jag-lovers.org
Excellent web-only resource. Run not-for-profit by volunteers, but with great on-line books and discussion forums for each model, including the E-type. It is possible to 'lurk' on the E-type forum without taking part if you just want to learn by reading what other people's car problems are and which solutions are suggested by the knowledgeable contributors.

www.xkedata.com
This website tracks surviving E-types. Add your car's data and the site gives excellent information on other E-types close to your own in the factory production run. It can also be used to run a history check of sorts, if a car you are examining is listed.

www.jdht.com
Holder of the official Jaguar archives on production numbers, build configuration and dispatch details, sometimes including first owner information. Sponsored by the Jaguar company and with a presence in the USA and UK, both of which issue Heritage Certificates confirming the originality of your car's major components on receipt of full ID plate details and proof of ownership.

Parts suppliers
David Manners, 991 Wolverhampton Road, Oldbury, Birmingham, B69 4RJ
Tel: + 44 (0)121 544 4040
www.jagspares.co.uk
Skilled workshop facilities as well as a parts supplier.

Martin Robey, Pool Road, Camphill Industrial Estate
Nuneaton, CV10 9AE
Tel: +44 (0)1203 386903
www.martinrobey.co.uk
The main supplier of E-type body panels, having invested in major sheet metal presses and other production facilities. Also holds large spares stocks for other models.

SNG Barratt Group Ltd
Addresses in UK, USA, Holland, France and Germany.
www.sngbarratt.com
Biggest and best? One of the oldest and most comprehensive spares sources for
E-types, including major remanufacturing capability for electrical parts, sub-assemblies,
castings such as bellhousings, fabricated parts such as bumpers and heater boxes,
etc. Much of what is sold by other suppliers comes originally from Barratts.

XKs Unlimited, 850 Fiero Lane, San Luis Obispo, CA 93401, USA
www.xks.com

Terry's Jaguar Parts, 117 E Smith Street, Benton, Il 62812, USA
www.terrysjag.com

Classic Jaguar, 9916 Hwy 290W, Austin, TX 78736, USA
www.classicjaguar.com

Useful books
Jaguar E-type, The Definitive History by Phillip Porter
Paperback: 256 pages ISBN: 0760303967
A magnum opus covering origins, development, launch, competition, sections
on each model and several major appendices. Some questionable data in the
appendices and not without its share of typos, etc, but really there is nothing that
compares with this. Worth every bit of its considerable cover price.

Original Jaguar E-type by Phillip Porter
Hardcover: 96 pages ISBN: 1870979125
More of a pictorial reference than a major written work for the three main series.
Useful for comparing a car you may be looking at and for checking the years when
various modifications and specification changes were introduced.

Jaguar E-type: 6 & 12 Cylinder Restoration Guide by Dr Thomas F Haddock
Paperback: 256 pages ISBN: 0760303967
(Currently out of print)
The Cinderella to Porter's Prince Charming? A dull black and white book with often
grainy photos, but a detail fetishist's dream volume. Acres of print on fastener and
clip specification, switch types, fixture changes down the years, and it would take
forever to learn. Commands very high prices due to its scarcity. Essential reading for
concours types, but not without occasional errors and best read in conjunction with
the JCNA concours guides.

Jaguar World Monthly Kelsey Publishing, www.kelsey.co.uk

17 Vital statistics
– essential data at your fingertips

Model	Month/year built period	Engine number prefix	Chassis number sequence (RHD)	Chassis number sequence (LHD)	Maximum speed
3.8 Conv.	03/61 – 10/64	R or RA	850	875	149
3.8 FHC	03/61 – 10/64	R or RA	860	885	150
4.2 S1 Conv.	10/64 – 12/67	7E	1E1001	1E10001	149
4.2 S1 FHC	10/64 - 12/67	7E	1E2001	1E30001	150
4.2 S1 2+2	03/66 - 10/68	7E	1E50001	1E75001	139
'S1.5' Conv.	12/67 - 10/68	7E	1E1864	1E15889	149
'S1.5' FHC	12/67 - 10/68	7E	1E21584	1E34250	150
'S1.5' 2+2	12/67 - 10/68	7E	1E50975	1E77645	139
4.2 S2 Conv.	10/68 - 09/70	7R	1R1001	1R7001	142 (126)*
4.2 S2 FHC	10/68 - 09/70	7R	1R20001	1R25001	143 auto 136 (128)*
4.2 S2 2+2	10/68 - 09/70	7R	1R35001	1R40001	139

* numbers in brackets indicate US specification model.
N.B. performance depends on gearing and varies between markets.

Technical specifications by model

3.8 Fixed Head Coupé – produced March 1961 to October 1964.
Engine: 6-cylinder, 87x106mm, 3781cc, CR 9:1 (8:1 optional), 3 x 2in SU Carbs,
rated 265bhp (gross) at 5500rpm. Max torque 260lb/ft at 4000rpm.
Transmission: axle ratio 3.31:1 (options 2.93, 3.27, 3.07, 3.54, 3.77, 4.09).
Overall gear ratios: 3.31, 4.25, 6.16, 11.18, reverse 11.18.
MPH/1000rpm in top gear: 23.0 (3.31), 21.5 (3.54), 24.8 (3.07), 26.0 (2.93) (running
on RS5 crossply tyres).
Suspension and brakes: IFS, torsion bars, anti-roll bar, wishbones and telescopic
dampers. IRS coil springs, lower wishbone/driveshaft, radius arms, telescopic
dampers and anti-roll bar. Rack and pinion steering. 11in disc brakes front and
10in rear. 6.40-15in tyres on 5in rim wire wheels; 5.5in rim rear wheels optional.
Dimensions: Wheelbase 8ft, front & rear track 4ft 2in, length 14ft 7.5in, width
5ft 5.25in, height 4ft.
Unladen weight: 24.25cwt.
Basic price: £1550.
Number produced[†]: 1798 RHD; 5781 LHD.

3.8 Open Two Seater – produced March 1961 to October 1964.
Specification as for FHC 3.8 apart from:
Height (soft top raised): 3ft 11in.
Unladen weight: 24cwt.
Basic price: £1480.
Number produced[†]: 942 RHD; 6885 LHD.

4.2 Fixed Head Coupé Series 1 and '1.5' – produced October 1964 to October 1968.
Specification as for 3.8 FHC apart from:
Engine: 6-cylinder, 92.07x106mm, 4235cc, CR 9:1 (8:1 optional), 3 x 2in SU Carbs, rated 265bhp (gross) at 5400rpm. Max torque 283lb/ft at 4000rpm.
Transmission: All synchro gearbox. Axle ratio 3.07:1 (options as per 3.8).
Overall gear ratios: 3.07, 3.90, 5.34, 8.23, reverse 9.45.
Unladen weight: 25cwt.
Basic price: £1648.
Number produced[†]: 1957 RHD; 5813 LHD.

4.2 Open Two Seater Series 1 and '1.5' – produced October 1964 to October 1968.
Specification as for 4.2 FHC apart from:
Height (soft top raised): 3ft 11in.
Unladen weight: 24.5cwt.
Basic price: £1568.
Number produced[†]: 1182 RHD; 8366 LHD.

4.2 2+2 Series 1 and '1.5' – produced March 1966 to October 1968.
Specification as for 4.2 FHC apart from:
Dimensions: Wheelbase 8ft 9in, front track and rear track 4ft 2.25in, length 15ft 4.5in, width 5ft 6in, height 4ft 2.5in.
Transmission: all synchro gearbox.
Axle ratio 3.07:1 (options as per FHC).
Overall gear ratios: 3.07, 4.07, 6.06, 9.33, reverse 10.71.
Unladen weight: 27.75cwt.
Basic price: £1857 (manual).
Number produced[†]: 1378 RHD; 4220 LHD.

4.2 Fixed Head Coupé Series 2 – produced October 1968 to September 1970.
Specification as for 4.2 Series 1 FHC apart from:
Unladen weight: 25.5cwt.
Width 5ft 6.25in.
Engine: emission controlled version 171bhp (DIN) at 4500rpm.
Max torque 230lb/ft at 2500rpm.
Basic price: £1740.
Number produced[†]: 1070 RHD; 3785 LHD.

4.2 Open Two Seater Series 2 – produced October 1968 to September 1970.
Specification as for 4.2 Series 2 FHC apart from:
Unladen weight: 25cwt.
Basic price: £1655.
Number produced[†]: 755 RHD; 7852 LHD.

4.2 2+2 (Series 2) – produced October 1968 to September 1970.
Specification as for 4.2 Series 2 FHC apart from:
Unladen weight: 28.25cwt.
Basic price: £1922 (Manual transmission).
Number produced[†]: 1040 RHD; 4286 LHD.

[†]Footnote: In the days of handwritten production, ledger discrepancies were known to creep in occasionally. There are various sources for the production numbers listed above. However, for the record, the JDHT-verified factory E-type production numbers are as follows:

Model	Conv.	FHC	2+2
3.8	7818	7663	–
4.2 S1	9551	7771	5586
4.2 S2	8641	4878	5329

The Essential Buyer's Guide™ series ...

Index